'A POET IN PARADISE'

LORD LINDSAY AND CHRISTIAN ART

SPONSORED BY GREAT NORTH EASTERN RAILWAY

AND ORIENT-EXPRESS HOTELS

ORIENT-EXPRESS
HOTELS

NICOLAS BARKER

HUGH BRIGSTOCKE AND TIMOTHY CLIFFORD

EDITED BY AIDAN WESTON-LEWIS

'A POET IN PARADISE'

LORD LINDSAY AND CHRISTIAN ART

NATIONAL GALLERY OF SCOTLAND

EDINBURGH

2000

Published by the Trustees of the National Galleries
of Scotland on the occasion of the exhibition 'A Poet in
Paradise': Lord Lindsay and Christian Art held at the National
Gallery of Scotland 25 August until 19 November 2000.

© National Galleries of Scotland 2000
ISBN 1 903278 10 4

Designed and typeset in Trinité by Dalrymple
Printed by BAS Printers, Over Wallop

Front cover illustration:
Attributed to Domenico Ghirlandaio
St Barbara Crushing her Infidel Father, with a Kneeling Donor
(cat.no.15)

Back cover illustration:
Detail from Ugolino di Nerio The Crucifixion
with the Virgin and St John the Evangelist
(cat.no.3)

Preface and Acknowledgements

The millennium concerns only one event and that is the two thousandth anniversary of the presumed date of the birth of Jesus Christ in Bethlehem of Judaea. This has nothing to do with domes – unless, I suppose, we are thinking of the Dome of the Rock – and is indisputably politically incorrect. At the National Galleries of Scotland, we have sought out a suitable exhibition of modest size and not over-whelming cost to celebrate this event and its subsequent cataclysmic effects on world history. Hopefully we have arrived at something entirely appropriate. For this exhibition charts the collection and collecting activities of a nineteenth-century Scottish nobleman and author who wrote a seminal and pioneering book about the evolution of early Italian art, the *Sketches of the History of Christian Art* (3 vols., London, 1847) and collected books and artefacts to inform and illustrate his researches, both as to Christian hagiography and iconography.

This small, sharply focused exhibition provides us with an excellent idea of what an enlightened Victorian nobleman – bookish, pedantic, incurably romantic – could acquire. As a rule, he was canny when buying pictures but profligate when buying books. The Lindsay family had homes in Lancashire and Aberdeenshire, but Lord Lindsay spent much of his time in Tuscany, especially later in life, staying at the very villa where Boccaccio wrote *The Decameron*. Lindsay bought objects rather casually, often of great rarity and intense beauty, all created by artists who were firmly believers of the Christian story, whether Gospel or Apocryphal. Of course, he also filled his houses with inherited family por-traits and pictures of family interest but they little concern us here. His taste was what one later associated with the taste of Wilhelm von Bode, sometime Director of the Kaiser-Friedrich-Museum in Berlin. He bought Renaissance bronzes, marbles, Italian maiolica and Flemish tapestries, as well as pictures. The problem in selecting and compiling this catalogue was to be satisfied that the art objects were definitely bought by Lord Lindsay rather than by his son or grandson, for his taste and erudition remained with the Lindsays, as indeed it still does today. Despite the regrettable dispersal of much of the outstanding library (which began less than a decade after Lord Lindsay's death), and a major sale of paintings in 1946, there is enough of Lord Lindsay's collection still available in Britain to allow a sizeable proportion to be reas-sembled here.

This exhibition is a rare treat for those of us who are passionate – like Ruskin or Pater, Eastlake or Morris, Berenson or Kenneth Clark – about that élite period of artistic creativity and patronage, the Italian *Quattrocento*. It is our firm intention to enthuse a very large public about these glorious pictures and artefacts.

The catalogue has been compiled by Hugh Brigstocke, formerly of the National Gallery of Scotland, whose knowledge of Lord Lindsay as a picture collector is encyclopaedic. The authority on Lindsay as a bibliophile is Nicolas Barker, formerly of the British Library, whose major book on the subject, *Bibliotheca Lindesiana*, published in 1978, documents in detail the history of the library and Lord Lindsay's activities as a book collector. I con-tributed the catalogue entries on the sculpture, textiles and ceramics. All the authors have been greatly indebted in a host of different ways to the editor of the catalogue, Aidan Weston-Lewis. We have also received invaluable and informative assistance from members of the Lindsay family.

The Gallery and the contributors to the catalogue gratefully acknowledge the assistance of the following in the realisation of this exhibition and its accompanying publication: Anthea Brigstocke; Alessandro Cecchi; Keith Christiansen; Kenneth Dunn; Everett Fahy; Dillian Gordon; Elspeth Hector; Tom Henry; John Hodgson; Peter Humfrey; Charles Janoray; Laurence B. Kanter; Vincent Kelly; Mauro Lucco; Jack MacKenzie; John Mallet; Sandra Martin; Clare Meredith; Nicholas Penny; Antonia Reeve; Francis Russell; Diana Scarisbrick; Luke Syson; Virginia Tandy; Jeremy Warren; Paul Williamson and Anne Young. We are particularly indebted to Stella Butler and the staff of the John Rylands University Library in Manchester for their enthusiastic support for this exhibition and for generously sanctioning the loan of an outstanding group of manuscripts from Lord Lindsay's library. Lisa Venturini kindly agreed to write the catalogue entry on the Francesco Botticini altarpiece at short notice, and in so doing to anticipate her forthcoming full publication of discoveries regarding its patronage and provenance. The exhibition could not have come about without the hard work and dedication of the staff of all departments of the National Galleries of Scotland. I am deeply indebted to Michael Clarke, the Keeper of the National Gallery of Scotland, for his patience and forbearance.

Last but by no means least, we would like gratefully to acknowledge the indispensable financial support we have received from our sponsors, Great North Eastern Railway and Orient-Express Hotels, and their President, James Sherwood.

TIMOTHY CLIFFORD
Director, National Galleries of Scotland

Sponsors' Foreword

This exhibition is the second at the National Gallery of Scotland being sponsored by the Great North Eastern Railway (GNER) and Orient-Express Hotels, both subsidiaries of Sea Containers Ltd. The railway was privatised in 1996 and has been operated by GNER since then. GNER has plans to increase its services between Scotland and London in the coming years while at the same time reducing travel time through the introduction of tilting trains and track improvements.

Orient-Express Hotels owns thirty-five luxury leisure properties throughout the world, including the Venice Simplon-Orient-Express train between London, Paris and Venice, the Hotel Cipriani and Palazzo Vendramin in Venice, the Villa San Michele in Florence and the Hotels Splendido and Splendido Mare in Portofino. It also owns the *Road to Mandalay* river cruise ship operating between Mandalay and the historic cities of Burma; the sixteenth-century Monasterio Hotel in Cusco, Peru and many other splendid hotels, tourist trains and restaurants on six continents.

We again congratulate Timothy Clifford and his team in bringing forth another seminal exhibition. GNER and Orient-Express Hotels are proud to be able to provide sponsorship.

JAMES B. SHERWOOD
President, Sea Containers Ltd.

Lord Lindsay and the Bibliotheca Lindesiana

NICOLAS BARKER

Alexander William Lindsay, known for most of his life simply as Lord Lindsay, was born on 16 October 1812 in the ancient Roman Tower of Muncaster Castle, his mother's old home. The castle stands on an independent spur high above the Esk, with Muncaster Fell to the east, the valley of the Esk to the south, and beyond its mouth at Ravenglas the open sea. It was in this ancient building, medieval but on still older foundations (Lindsay found Roman gold coins under its flagstones), surrounded by a remote and beautiful valley, that he began his childhood. 'I have scarce one attachment or pursuit', he wrote many years later, 'of which I cannot trace the germ at least to my residence at Muncaster. There I drank in that reverence for antiquity of whatever sort, architectural, genealogical, historical, traditional; that love for learning and burning thirst of knowledge, and that love and sympathy for mountains, glens and clear streams that have afforded me so much delight through life.'

All too soon, the family had to leave this paradise. Lord Muncaster died, and a complex succession meant that much of the property had to be sold. Lindsay's father James, the future 7th Earl of Balcarres and still later 24th Earl of Crawford, and his family had to leave, and went to stay with their Caledon cousins in the south. James was on bad terms with his father, who had left Scotland for his wife's inherited estate of Haigh Hall, near Wigan, Lancashire, which was thus no refuge now. All that was rescued from Muncaster was the library, going back to the seventeenth century. This was just as well, for the even more ancient library of the Lindsays had fallen on sad days. Apart from a single medieval manuscript, the *Roman de la Rose* written in 1323 for Christian, daughter of Sir William de Lindsay and Ada, daughter of John Baliol, King of Scotland, this was the creation of two remarkable brothers, David, Lord Edzell (1551–1610) and John, Lord Menmuir (1552–1598). Their books were the foundation of the large library (by the standards of the time) that Lord Menmuir's son, David, Lord Balcarres (1587–1640) built up. His books covered almost every branch of literature and learning, and he had them specially bound and stamped with the Lindsay crest or arms, and the family motto 'Astra Castra Numen Lumen Munimen' ('The stars, my camp; God my light and defence'). Later generations suffered for their loyalty to the Crown and the Stewart dynasty. It was not until Alexander, the 6th Earl of Balcarres (1752–1825), whose marriage brought into the family the estates around Haigh in Lancashire –

then thought barren but later found to be rich in underground coal – that it was possible to begin to rebuild the family fortunes.

Absence and neglect had wrought irremediable harm to the Lindsay library, and it was to be Lord Lindsay's special delight to retrieve books that the family had once owned. The *Roman de la Rose* manuscript mentioned above was bought back, improbably, from the Smets sale in New York in May 1868; he found the 1538 Sarum Primer that had belonged to Katherine Campbell, mother of David and John Lindsay, in Edinburgh in November 1856; and most of the books still surviving from the first Lord Balcarres's library were similarly reacquired. Meantime, however, the young Lindsay was acquiring the passion for reading that was to last the rest of his life. It was followed soon after by an equal delight in writing: poetry, history, an English grammar; three little volumes still survive, entitled in script like type 'William's Works for Children. By William Lindsay. Second Edition revised and improved. 1821. (Price One Shilling)'. A third passion, buying books, came simultaneously. In April 1821, when he was still only eight, his mother had written to him: 'I have no objection to your spending your shilling in the purchase of a book but it must not be a *silly* one.'

A year later, Lindsay's parents finally moved to Haigh Hall, and he was sent to school at Mr Rusden's, Leith Hill Place, near Dorking. Mr Rusden was one of those rare schoolmasters who teach not only the grammar but the love of languages. As Lindsay later recalled: 'He made such enthusiasts of us that I for one, nor was I singular, I believe, obtained permission to join in the lessons of the class above me, on the condition of preparing them in play hours. Hence my love for Horace.' As well as the classics, he soon knew by heart long passages of English poetry, Shakespeare, Spenser, Pope's Homer and Scott's *The Lay of the Last Minstrel*. There were occasional excursions to London, to stay with his greataunt, Lady Anne. Lady Caledon took him to see the sights, 'the Wappitee and the Reindeer and the Laplanders', the current attraction at the Egyptian Hall, and in the evening to the theatre in Drury Lane, where they saw *The School for Scandal* and *The Golden Axe, or Harlequin and the Gold in the Fairy Lake*. 'I have bought a work called, *Galt's Pictures Historical and Biographical of English, Scottish and Irish History*', he told his mother. Which, one wonders, of all the London booksellers received the first order of a customer for which three generations of the trade were to contend?

Fig.1 · Attributed to William Barclay Junior (1797-1859)
Alexander William, Lord Lindsay, aged seventeen
Private Collection

At Haigh during the holidays there was much to absorb Lindsay's inquisitive young mind. There were fascinating building works in hand; heraldry, the forerunner of genealogy, began to interest him; and there was Mr Brown, the Wigan bookseller, generous in providing old books and even the loan of a printing press. 'Pray, dear Mama, do not forget my bookcase', he wrote home. 'You may depend upon it my dear child your bookcase shall be ready for you – but if you have 200!! volumes I am afraid the bookcase will not hold them all', his mother replied. Unabashed, his next letter boasted: 'I have lately got a most beautiful Euripides, 6 vols for 7 shillings with various readings and uncut.' In 1825 his grandfather died, and that autumn he went to Eton, stopping at the London booksellers on the way. At first his tutor's reports were encouraging; he was 'very studious indeed, reading something or other always, diligent, attentive, and very well behaved', only 'He does not enter into the sports and games of others much, and there is a singularity about him'. This prescient phrase betokened a trouble that was to dog his youth and early manhood, a sense of otherness with which he did not fully come to terms until his marriage. He was wretchedly bullied, and asked in vain to be removed. Eventually, transferred to a dame's house and with his own tutor, school became more tolerable, but life began in the holidays, as he later remembered:

'I began collecting in a small way in 1826, shortly after going to Eton, and at the same time endeavoured to prepare myself for the work of future years by the study of the science of bibliography in such books as I could afford to buy or could get access to: Dr. Clarke's Bibliographical Dictionary was my constant companion. Dibdin's writings, in particular, made me for the time a thorough bibliomaniac. I met Dr Dibdin once at a friend's house, and although he discoursed on matters very foreign to the subject of libraries – it was at the time of the Reform Bill of 1832, and he was a Rabid Radical – I remember the sight I had of him with pleasure. I had distant glimpses of other collectors, and frequent opportunities of gazing on books of beauty and value, in the great room of Messrs Payne and Foss in Pall Mall, a literary Rialto, where the Spencers, Hebers, and Grenvilles were wont to congregate, and where, while collating, in particular, by permission of those courteous bibliopoles, the poems of Simonides, which it was my ambition to edit, in the Anthology of 1495, I watched them from the corner come and go, like ghosts and phantoms, who might have noticed me had I taken the initiative and ventured to speak to them ... I collected in this way as many books (chiefly classical and philological) as sufficed to cover an entire wall of my room at Eton; and among them were a few volumes not unworthy to hold their place even in our present library.'

In March 1827 Lindsay compiled his first catalogue of pictures, prints, medals and books, the family's and his own, neatly written in a series of pocket-books, all adorned with his signature in calligraphic form, imitated from those in his ancestors' books. By then there were almost five hundred books to be listed, among them a fifteenth-century French manuscript Book of Hours, five contemporary printed texts, a long range of classical texts and bibles, as well as one or two books from the Balcarres library, including a Latin bible of 1624, recently retrieved from a bookseller in Dumfries. In 1829 he left Eton (fig.1), and the next two years were to be spent abroad, first in Paris, and then in Italy. He was bowled over by the Louvre and the Bibliothèque Royale, saw M. Erard's famous Claudes, and haunted the book-stalls on the quais, where he found 'sixteen of the Elzevir Republics, Boileau's copy, neat, with his arms stamped on the back, for 4d a piece, and carried them all home with me, distributed in my hat, my hands, and my various pockets'. His father, busy rebuilding Haigh, was alarmed, and discharged a familiar warning. 'The name of the Painter ought to give no additional value to the picture', he wrote, and 'a volume can claim no additional value (beyond its correct text) because it may be printed by Caxton or any other early printer ... It is some time since your family has produced a first rate man', he ended, urging him not to 'engross your mind too much with solitary and unprofitable amusements'.

Lindsay bore this with equanimity, and his subsequent letters home dealt less with such things and more with matters social. He had met Lady Mary Crawford, the sister of the 22nd Earl of Crawford, who had died in 1808 with no near male kin. The family papers had descended to her, awakening all Lindsay's genealogical interest. In the spring his parents joined him, and soon plans were forming for a longer journey. Lord Hardwicke provided letters of introduction to the Hanoverian minister in Rome, with access to the Vatican and the Pope: 'He is not the Pope to whom I was presented who was a very civil good man, but I hear excellent accounts of his present holiness.' Soon Lindsay was over the Simplon Pass, captivated by the scenery, the sunrises 'where a thousand little clouds of bright orange

Fig.2 · Attributed to Christina Robertson (1796–1854)
Colonel James Lindsay
Private Collection

Fig.3 · British School, nineteenth century
Anne Trotter, Mrs Lindsay, wife of Colonel James Lindsay
Private Collection

colour filled in streaks the whole horizon gradually fading away at the extremities'. Like Ruskin, he was struck by the 'peculiar and highly beautiful brown pink colour' of the mountains. Milan, the Brera and the Biblioteca Ambrosiana delighted him, as did Bergamo, Brescia, Verona, Vicenza, Padua and the Scrovegni Chapel. Venice, 'where we had two gondolieri out one fine night to sing Tasso', and St Mark's ('more like a mosque than a Christian church') were followed by Florence and Fra Angelico, then Rome, where he visited St Peter's and met Lady Mary Crawford again, and finally Naples and all the places around. He returned via Pisa, where he ordered a marble chimney-piece for his father's new Haigh Hall, and Florence, with a last vision of Vallombrosa in sunset, 'and then the gloaming, so sweet so delicious', with fireflies, 'a thousand stars dashing among the trees ... and then the approach of night, star after star appearing'.

Back home, he went to Trinity College, Cambridge, where he founded a Scottish Club and met Tennyson. But this made rather less impact on him than his first journey to Scotland to visit his cousin James Lindsay (fig.2) and his wife Anne (fig.3), daughter of Sir Coutts Trotter, with whom Lindsay struck up a warm and lasting friendship. He played with their children, Coutts and Margaret ('Min'), and fell in love with the old house at Balcarres, the landscape and the views across the Firth of Forth. They in turn fell for his 'Scotomania' – it was a new Lindsay, full of energy and charm, who delighted them with his tales of the past and the family's part in it. It was then that the ideal of the Bibliotheca Lindesiana was formed, a library for the family in its widest sense and all its friends. Then a miracle happened that

turned a dream into reality. Lady Mary Crawford died, naming Lindsay her general heir, which brought not only the deeds that he had coveted, but two houses, a mass of personal property and a library, 'books of all sizes many of them as I saw by a hasty glance works on Scottish history', as well as old family documents. Most important of all, the bequest gave him financial independence, freedom to indulge his genius: 'all my Bibliomania so long pent up in some recess of my heart has gushed out again and I am dreaming night and day about the Library.' He wrote to his mother:

'I wish I could impart to you a tenth of the pleasure I have in thinking about, and shall have in arranging, contemplating and adding to our Library. I do not intend getting *flash* editions, but good ones, for use and consultation, not for shew; shew books and fine editions are very well in their way, but what I wish to form is a *reading* Library, a Library equally fit for the studious and the elegant squires. Ours, such as it is, is an excellent one, but I will make it *super-excellent*, not a Lord-Spencer collection, but a useful one, with so much of the ornamental as to relieve the mind and eye when tired with standard and grave literature.'

The 1830s was a wonderful decade in which to begin to realise this ideal. The library of Richard Heber (1773–1833), the greatest book collector of his age, came up for sale, and the range of books that he had collected, ancient and modern, corresponded very fully with Lindsay's tastes: literature, history, genealogy, geography and travel, the classics, theology and encyclopaedias – all this made an admirable foundation. Self-denying, Lindsay concentrated on the useful rather than the rare, even passing by early editions of Sir David Lindsay's verse, fearful lest 'I might have lost myself in a bibliomaniacal rut, and never afterwards escaped from it'. Yet bibliomania would out. Lady Mary's legacy settled and, down in London, he strolled out one day in April 1834 to a bookseller's: 'It was a glorious *mine* of old books that I sprung', he wrote in great excitement to his cousin James:

'The man had just the day before yesterday got in a number of old books, and I take it I am the first Bibliomaniac who visited the shop since their arrival. I purchased above 40 volumes from him which I selected out of the miscellaneous contents of the shop, diving into every corner and in *such* a state of nervous agitation, jealous of every one who entered the place lest with a Bibliomaniac's eye he should discover my intended booty and snap it up before I could finally secure it. Of these books many I bought because they were *useful* and valuable to a Library on account of their *intrinsic merit* independent of rarity or cheapness ... others were really rejoicing to the eye of a lover of antiquity, fifteen and sixteen hundreders, in capital condition and more than one very valuable as well as curious. The great gun was the Latin Bible printed by Coburger at Norimbergae in 1479, a tremendous folio, bound in the original wood boards with clasps and in the finest possible condition, quite perfect, large broad margins, beautiful gothic type, white and spotless throughout: oh my dear James, it is a glorious book!'

His mother could still cast him down by protesting at 'Spanish which nobody scarcely can read', his misery assuaged by his father's gift of *Cronicas y memorias de los reyes de Castilla* 1779–87, 'a magnificent copy on large paper'. But soon Heber's copy of the Icelandic *Edda*, a favourite text, was followed by Nonnus's *Dionysiaca*, 'a beautiful manuscript of the Bhagavat Ghita, in Sanskrit, with 17 drawings', and then 'I picked up Morrison's Chinese Bible ... for a mere trifle, 21 small volumes'. He made up for abstinence in the matter of David Lindsay by buying Heber's *Spanish Chronicles*, and one day 'when in Bohn's in came Beckford, the author of "Vathek", and talked for a long while most satisfactorily'. He was seventy-five, Lindsay twenty-two, yet they had much in common, a precocious taste for books and pictures, a natural bent for collecting, and an invincible disposition to romance, even if Beckford's career showed all the snares that a bibliomaniacal Circe might set in the path that his young acquaintance was determined to avoid.

By then Lindsay had further plans for travel, with his young friend William Ramsay, to the Holy Land, and then for a longer sojourn in Italy. The journey to the Near East, to monasteries where 'Several leaves of a Syriac Bible alighted at our feet as we rode up to the gate', was saddened by the sudden death of Ramsay, but led to Lindsay's first book, *Letters on Egypt, Edom and the Holy Land*, published in 1838. This led him in turn to take up the 'interminable Clan History I made at Cambridge for my little Minnie, alias Margaret, and Coutts Lindsay', which he finished the following year. By then James and Anne were enlarging Balcarres, and to avoid the disturbance (and for economy) they went abroad for a long time. Lindsay could not wait to follow them, and there was a happy reunion at Rome, where he had all the children painted by George Richmond. They travelled all over Italy 'in gypsey style, Anne riding, James and I walking alter-

nately', and discovered 'the ancient Italian painters together', the ideas that were to become *Sketches of the History of Christian Art* forming in his head as they went. Next year, Lindsay went again, this time accompanied by Coutts, and forearmed with Masselli's edition of Vasari, 'in 2 large vols with notes, telling what has become of the different frescoes and works of art he describes, and mentioning others which he omits'. While in Rome, 'I picked up a delightful book, De Natalibus's Lives of the Saints printed about the end of the 15th century and giving all the legends in their unadorned simplicity – the very thing I wanted and had long been searching for as a vademecum in my fresco explorations'.

They set off, taking in every place, large or small, between Rome and Florence, where Lindsay said goodbye to Coutts. He stayed on, working in the Biblioteca Laurenziana as well as the Uffizi, then set off for the north, revisiting all the cities of the Po valley, Venice (where he dwelt for 'hours in St Mark's'), on to Munich, a glimpse of the 'Vienna Genesis', with its late classical illustrations, to Lübeck and finally home via Bruges and Van Eyck. He had been away ten months, and now, with a wealth of visual experience to add to his reading, sat down to write it up. He was alone at Haigh; James and Anne, kind critics by post, were wintering abroad again. He was also engaged in the complicated genealogical research that was to bear fruit in 1848, when the family's claim to the ancient Earldom of Crawford, briefly theirs in the sixteenth century, was finally upheld. *Sketches of the History of Christian Art* and *Lives of the Lindsays* were published in 1847, to respectful notices. Small wonder that Lindsay, in a fever of intellectual activity and with an internal doubt of his sanity that went back to his Eton troubles, was near breakdown. Antoine Petroz, successor to the inventor of homoeopathy, Samuel Hahnemann, provided the cure he needed. Liberated from his fears, he felt able to confess his long felt but unspoken love for his cousin Margaret (fig.4), to find it reciprocated. It was a surprise even to James and Anne, but unclouded happiness followed their marriage on 23 July 1846.

These events were the climacteric in Lindsay's life, and marked a turning point in the history of the Bibliotheca Lindesiana. Throughout the previous twenty years, his father had been building up a great business, as well as the new house at Haigh. Judicious purchase of abutting land and new methods of mining the coal that lay beneath it had increased the family's wealth. 'Lord Bal', as he was always known, built railways

- themselves a major consumer of coal – to move it, especially to the port of Liverpool, and made steel for rails and locomotives. The new speed of communication accelerated this industrial growth; it also accelerated the growth of the Bibliotheca Lindesiana, now that the penny post could take a letter from Wigan to London and get the answer back within the day. To Lindsay, wealth and opportunity carried with them a duty, and libraries conferred an obvious benefit on humanity.

'What may be less open to observation is the fact (which grows ever more and more on my own apprehension) that a choice and well ordered private Library exercises a most ennobling influence on the family which possesses it, and through such families upon society. The like may be said of pictures and works of art – indeed of any intellectual heritage, duly prized ... It is for this reason that, while public libraries are the glory of nations and blessings to humanity, private libraries are, I venture to think, of equal value in the great account – provided only that large and liberal hearts preside over their collection, custody and communication.'

With this faith, and a greater understanding – brought by marriage and the responsibilities that came to him – of the extent of the family fortune, Lindsay determined on a great expansion of the family library. The increase in spending on books, deliberately begun in the mid-1850s, must be seen as an investment in the moral and intellectual welfare of the family as substantial as the material investment made by his father earlier.

Old acquaintances in the book trade – Henry Bohn, Willis and Sotheran, Joseph Lilly – now began to receive larger and more frequent orders. Lilly supplied a copy of Bartholomaeus Anglicus, printed for Caxton in Cologne in 1471 before he began printing himself; two manuscripts of the *Shah-Nameh*; the first English Froissart (1525); and he offered a complete set of De Bry's *Voyages*, only to discover that there was a better set already at Haigh. Lindsay's explanation, and a subsequent essay on the collation of sixteenth-century bibles, provoked the astounded bookseller to exclaim: 'I must say that as regards collation etc. etc. your Lordship *excels me in my own profession !!!*' Early English bibles, accounts of discoveries, grammars, music, the first editions of Chapman's Homer and the *Etymologies* of Isidore, poured in from Lilly. Molini, an old friend from Florence, supplied books on the arts, ancient and modern, topography and genealogy, and a complete set of the *Acta Sanctorum* from

1643 to the present day in 52 volumes for 555 scudi (£125). T. & W. Boone, booksellers to the British Museum, supplied occasional books. David Nutt delivered, from Friedländer in Berlin, a copy of the 'Columbus Letter', printed in Rome in 1493. Another Italian bookseller, Giovanni Gancia, supplied the *editio princeps* of Homer (1488) and the *Divina Comedia* of 1481, with all the engravings by Baccio Baldini after Botticelli; this was cheap, because the plates had been pasted in face downwards, but, as Gancia pointed out, 'they are when unpasted most beautiful'.

But of all the beneficiaries of this new campaign, the greatest was the then almost unknown Bernard Quaritch (1819–1899), who had set up shop in Castle Street (the present Charing Cross Road) only in 1847. In 1852 he issued a catalogue of philology, from which Lindsay bought nine books, mainly Norse, but also including a trilingual Basque-Spanish-Latin dictionary. This led to further orders for books of the same sort, all promptly executed. Lindsay extended the range to Polish and Bohemian genealogy, and a coloured copy of Gruner's *Fresco Decorations*. In May 1858 there was an important sale in Augsburg, followed in June by that of Robert Daly, Bishop of Cashel. Both included copies of Gutenberg's bible, then known as the 'Mazarine' since it had been first identified in the cardinal's library. Lindsay gave commissions to Quaritch, who set off for Augsburg. He did not buy the bible, nor all the other books ordered, but he showed himself energetic and judicious, refusing to buy less than satisfactory copies. So Lindsay gave him the commission for Bishop Daly's bible. Competition was stiff, but the outcome, Quaritch felt, demanded one of the then new telegrams. The Electric and International Telegraph Company was not quite equal to the task: I BOUGHT THE MARINE FOR FIVE HUNDRED NINETY FIVE POUNDS SHALL I SEND IT I DECLINE TAKING ANY COMMISSION, it ran. Lindsay had no difficulty in decoding it.

Thereafter, Quaritch had the lion's share of the Bibliotheca Lindesiana orders, and not long after came the opportunity to extend it into the field of medieval manuscripts, hardly represented so far. Guglielmo Libri (1803–1869), mathematician, revolutionary, book collector and thief, excelled in all the fields he touched. Having made France too hot to hold him, he had found distinguished supporters in England, where he made a living by selling the books he had acquired, legitimately as well as nefariously. The extent of his misdeeds was then unknown, but

Fig.4
British School
nineteenth century
Margaret (Min) Lindsay, wife of Lord Lindsay
Private Collection

Quaritch was rightly suspicious of his optimistic cataloguing when his manuscripts were offered for sale in March 1859. The immediate outcome was a limited success, thanks in no small measure to Quaritch's initiative. Lindsay lost a Greek gospel-book and an eighth-century manuscript of St Cyprian (his son retrieved the latter for the library over thirty years later), but got a fine ninth-century Carolingian Gospels (cat.no.55). When the box in which Quaritch had carefully packed the books arrived, he was delighted.

'The Cassianus (cat.no.60) is also a very choice MS – the illumination being in the finest style of the art of the time it was executed; and he is greatly pleased to possess the MS, having always felt a great interest in the monks of the Egyptian Desert with whom Cassian records his colloquies. The Latin Gospels (cat.no.55) is a most beautiful specimen of Carlovingian calligraphy, and the portrait of St Luke [in fact, St Mark] a valuable and admirably preserved specimen of the peculiar painting of the school founded or rather reinvigorated by Charlemagne ... But none of these are more interesting (in its peculiar way) than the tattered and battered Homilies of the 8th century (cat.no.54), a most interesting relic of the early church, and which will stand well at the commencement of the series of service books and liturgies in Lord L's possession.'

It is a measure of his intellectual grasp that over the next four months Lindsay moved on to acquire a notable series of natural history books, as well as important additions to his collection of early romances of chivalry (the books that turned Don Quixote's head). More of these came at the Solar sale next year in Paris, but the real triumph there was a different kind of book, the first printed encyclopaedia. Quaritch's report was vivid:

'Lot 784 Catholicon, on Vellum, 1460 – was put on the table. M. Techener said "Dix mille francs, marchand"; I stood staggered, the commissaire priseur looked at me, and so did probably others, Techener's bid sounded like Napoleon's "je les ai enfin, ces Anglais"; well, the 10,000 shot went into our ranks, and as I stated the volley shook my nerves for a while, until my blood came back, and I deliberately said "cinquante", from there the fire of bids was slowly but steadily kept up until at 12,450 the lot was knocked down to me, to the consternation of the immense concourse of French amateurs.

'Your Lordship must excuse my excentricity in comparing sales to battles, but really if balls were flying round me in good earnest, victory could not interest me more than a victory like the present, obtained for your Lordship and with your Lordship's good money.'

In the very same month, Lindsay also laid out £390 on the very rare Missal of the York use, printed in Rouen in 1516. Earlier, Thomas Kerslake, whom Lindsay dubbed 'the eccentric bookseller of Bristol', had provided the thirteenth-century manuscript Sarum Missal (cat.no.57), bought from 'a church near Torquay', which again pleased him on several grounds:

'It is a very interesting MS intrinsically, and in point of calligraphy and illumination leaves nothing to be desired. The miniatures are full of spirit, extremely interesting for the history of English art, and in excellent preservation. The drawing of the extremities, so seldom given with any approach to shapeliness in MSS of such early date, is singularly good. The volume has a particular interest too, as remarked by Mr Kerslake, in having preserved its original character and appearance intact.'

Other important manuscripts came later: in 1861, a twelfth-century copy of Peter Lombard's *Commentary on the Psalms* from a Rhenish monastery, in a slightly later jewelled binding, was bought from Boone (cat.no.56); the beautiful Malatesta manuscript of Nicolas de Lyra, also from Boone, in 1866 (cat.no.59); in 1869, the fine French thirteenth-century psalter bearing the name 'Royne Jehanne', who Lindsay thought (too hopefully) might be the daughter of King John, who married Alexander II of Scotland (cat.no.58); and in August 1872, from Quaritch, the little Flemish Book of Hours, twice inscribed by Mary Queen of Scots (cat.no.61), to add to a printed Hours, given to Mary by Catherine de Medicis, and by her to her uncle the Cardinal de Guise, that Lindsay had bought the previous March.

All these paled by comparison with what Boone, writing on 19 June 1868, described as 'the *finest Illuminated Book*, ever offered for Sale', the six volumes (each in contemporary but not uniform bindings) of the Missal of Cardinal Pompeo Colonna, for which he asked and received the vast sum of £1,500 (cat.no.62). This masterpiece of Italian Renaissance art elicited a warm response: 'Lord Lindsay has carefully examined the MSS volumes which Mr Boone has been good enough to offer him, and he cordially confesses that Mr Boone's estimate of their beauty ... is not exaggerated.' Pausing only to enquire whether the first volume, which contained most decoration, could be bought separately (Boone wisely refused), he agreed to buy it,

Figs.5 & 6 · Unknown photographer
View of the exterior of Dunecht, Aberdeenshire
The Drawing Room at Dunecht

paying over six months. 'I am happy to think', wrote Boone, 'that the splendid Colonna Manuscripts will find a resting place where they will be so well appreciated, and as regards payment I am content to leave it to your Lordship's convenience and pleasure'.

So the library grew and prospered, while Lindsay directed its progress. In 1869, Lord Bal died and Lindsay succeeded him as 25th Earl of Crawford. The library continued to fill his days, and the sheer volume of correspondence that it involved – let alone a scholarship that ranged from theology and comparative religion, through philosophy, history in all its branches, the documents of the discovery and mapping of the world, all the languages and literature of the world (his own range covered Europe and some oriental languages), to genealogy, natural science and, above all, art and its history – would have been far beyond a man of less ability. Nonetheless, he found time to take an active part in the direction of the Wigan Coal & Iron Company, to commission a great house from G.E. Street on the Aberdeenshire estate of Dunecht that Lord Bal had bought him (figs. 5 & 6), and to find a villa in Florence, where he and his beloved Min resorted when the smoke and grime from the chimneys of Wigan became intolerable. He even found time to write on the subjects in which he was expert, the succession to the Earldom of Mar, the Etruscan language that led him to explore the primal roots of language in *The Creed of Japhet*, and even to revert to his first muse – translating Horace and writing the epic *Argo*, published in 1876 with a long autobiographical prelude that provides this exhibition with its title.

But in 1880 he died, quite suddenly, and the Bibliotheca Lindesiana changed tack. Ludovic, his son and successor as the 26th Earl, was a man of no less ability, who added astronomy and the abstract sciences to complete the library's scope. It had grown from 6,000 books in 1834 to over 30,000, and the 26th Earl continued its growth, employing a librarian (he was himself an authority on library classification) and adding notable medieval manuscripts and early printed books in the great sales of the 1880s, as well as the usual mass of current works. But the depression that had forced those sales eventually caught up with the greatest of all the private libraries formed in the nineteenth century. Some of the best printed books had to be sold in 1887 and 1889, and the manuscripts went *en bloc* to the great new John Rylands Library at Manchester in 1901, the remainder being largely dispersed later. But his great vision for it remains in the vast report on the purpose and scope of the Bibliotheca Lindesiana that Lindsay had written for Ludovic, in whom, aged fourteen, he had begun to discern a fellow feeling (fig.7). He wrote from Florence:

'I have written you this letter, my dear Ludovic, not from Haigh or Dunecht, but from our villa at San Domenico below Etruscan Fiesole, where I hope ere many days to hail your advent from England ... Turning northwards, I see from our garden, above us, and below the brow of Fiesole, the long line of the terraced gardens and villa of the Medici, the work of Michelozzo, where Cosimo and Lorenzo and their less worthy successors lived and died, and where the Platonic Academy held its meetings immortalised by Landino. I little thought in my boyhood when Cosimo and Lorenzo were the object of my worship at Eton, that I should one day dwell beside their favourite San Domenico, look up at their villa, and point to my son a parallel and a moral from their history. The parallel is this: what commerce did, directly, for the Medici in the fifteenth century, commerce has done indirectly for our own family in the nineteenth. In the days of Cosimo, with above thirty baronies at our back and thousands of vassals ready to ride at our command, even against the royal banners, our revenues in actual coin (even including those received from the customs of sea-ports) were comparatively small, and would not have availed for the collection of books or pictures, even had the taste for such gear existed in those days in feudal Scotland. But now, when those thirty baronies are to ourselves as things of the past, and we have, as a Spaniard would say, but one "hat" to boast of, at least in Scotland, the growth of trade has, by a strange recompense, afforded us, through the possession of coalfields in England, the means of doing what our more powerful ancestors, the contemporaries of Cosimo, could not have compassed – of building up our old Library after the example of the Medici, and in the mode they would themselves have acted upon had they been now living.'

NOTE: The documents on which this account is based are the family and library letters relating to the Bibliotheca Lindesiana, the majority of them currently on deposit at the National Library of Scotland. The longer extracts are from the 'Library Letter', written by Lord Lindsay for his son, referred to in the last paragraph above.

Lord Lindsay and the 'Sketches of the History of Christian Art'

HUGH BRIGSTOCKE

Alexander William, the eldest son of James, later 24th Earl of Crawford and 7th Earl of Balcarres, and of Maria Pennington, heiress to the 1st Baron Muncaster, was born at Muncaster Castle, situated high above the River Esk in Cumbria, on 16 October 1812. By the time he succeeded his father as 25th Earl of Crawford and inherited the family home at Haigh Hall, Wigan, in 1869, he had acquired a very considerable reputation both as a scholar and writer and also as a collector of books and works of art.

The ambition to write a book on the early Italian painters was first conceived by Lord Lindsay in 1839, during a tour of Italy which he made with his cousin Colonel James Lindsay and his wife Anne (figs. 2 & 3). James and Anne were to become Lord Lindsay's closest friends and the recipients of his most informative travel letters; their home became the young scholar's principal refuge and in 1846 their daughter Margaret became his wife. Their other children were Coutts, who inherited his grandfather's baronetcy, trained as a painter under Ary Scheffer and started the Grosvenor Gallery; Mary Anne, who married Robert Holford of Westonbirt, one of the richest picture collectors of his time; and Robert James, who became Baron Wantage and also formed an important art collection.

The purpose of this essay is to explain the significance of Lindsay's major contribution to art historical literature, the *Sketches of the History of Christian Art*, published in 1847. But first we must examine the context within which he formed a taste for early Italian painting and sculpture, then still highly unfashionable. From the time of the Renaissance until the late eighteenth century, when revolution and war wrought profound changes in Europe, the study of early Italian art had been almost exclusively the preserve of scholarly but provincial antiquarians whose labours went largely unnoticed elsewhere. Paradoxically, the first significant turning point in the critical rediscovery of the Primitives came not from these manifestations of local pride, but from the obsession of foreign travellers with the twin peaks of artistic achievement, classical antiquity and the Italian High Renaissance, reflecting the ideas of the sixteenth-century Italian writer Giorgio Vasari, with his progressive view of stylistic development in art. For it was within this neoclassical framework that a well connected French scholar, Jean-Baptiste Séroux d'Agincourt (1730–1814), began a survey entitled *Histoire de l'Art par les monuments depuis sa décadence au IVe siècle jusqu'à son renouvellement au XVIe siècle*, which was completed in 1789 but not published until 1810–23. It had involved employing numerous artists to make engraved copies of antique and medieval art, including those elements within medieval art that linked classical antiquity to the revival of classical values in the Renaissance. Séroux d'Agincourt was a friend of Johann Winckelmann, the great German historian of Greek and Roman art and the archetypal apologist for Neoclassicism. He also knew both Horace Walpole, whom he visited at Strawberry Hill, and Charles Townley, the celebrated collector of antique marbles. It seems that he conceived his *Histoire ...* as the visual adjunct to Edward Gibbon's *Decline and Fall of the Roman Empire* (1776–88), a seminal historical survey that had equated Rome's downfall with the rise of Christianity.[1] Yet ironically, his enormous corpus of engraved reproductions also served to draw attention to the residual impact of Paleo-Christian art, Byzantine mosaics and the expressive power of some fourteenth- and fifteenth-century Florentine painters. Indeed many of the young artists who worked for Séroux d'Agincourt, including John Flaxman, Jean-Baptiste Wicar from Lille, and the Dutch painter Humbert de Superville, became sympathetic admirers of the Primitives. This group also included William Young Ottley (1771–1836), who later formed his own collection, wrote a book on the subject (*The Italian School of Design*, 1823), and was probably the first to refer to the Italian Primitives in a descriptive rather than pejorative sense; and the French aristocratic Catholic, Paillot de Montabert (1771–1849), author of the *Dissertation sur les peintures du moyen âge et sur celles qu'on a appelées gothiques* (1812). Although still writing within the neoclassical tradition of Winckelmann, Paillot de Montabert introduced a more romantic approach to medieval art, focused on its spiritual and moral power.[2]

Indeed, the second stage in the rehabilitation of early Italian art had already begun with the arrival in Rome in 1810 of the German Nazarene artists. This movement sought to revive the Christian spirit of the early Italian painters and was based on a romantic admiration for Gothic civilisation, medieval chivalry and religious sentiment. The concept of Christian art as a spiritual force replaced the idea of primitive art as a link in a historical chain. The Nazarenes inspired a new generation of German writers, including Carl von Rumohr (a Catholic convert) and J.D. Passavant, who had himself been a Nazarene painter and later wrote a monograph on Raphael (1839) which emphasised the spir-

Fig.7 · Camille Silvy (1835–1910)
Photograph of Lord Lindsay with his son, Ludovic, c.1865

itual purity of his home background in Urbino and of his work in Umbria. Charles Eastlake, who had first visited Rome as a young artist preoccupied with the Antique, and who later became Keeper and then Director of the National Gallery in London, was quick to appreciate the shift in art-historical taste and wrote a highly influential review (*Quarterly Review*, June 1840) of Passavant's book. This in turn inspired the Scottish Jacobite historian James Dennistoun to write his *Memoirs of the Dukes of Urbino* (1851). Of the British artists in Rome, William Dyce probably had the closest contact with Overbeck and his associates.

By the 1830s enthusiasm for the religious sentiment and expressive power of early Christian art was being fuelled by the French Catholic writer A.F. Rio, whose influential *De La Poésie Chrétienne* (1836) denounced the paganism associated with High Renaissance painting. No longer were the early Italian artists to be judged for their place in the historical development of Italian art, but according to a moral code based on subject-matter, feeling and style. He was contemptuous of the art of the schismatic Byzantines, underestimated Cimabue and Nicola Pisano, and regarded Romano-Christian art as decadent. Links with classical antiquity were of no concern. He concentrated his attention on the Germano-Christian tradition emanating from the Carolingian era and the early medieval manuscript illuminators; on the art of Guido da Siena, especially his celebrated *Madonna* in San Domenico; on Giotto at Assisi; the Campo Santo in Pisa, and Orcagna in Florence. He drew a sharp distinction between those fifteenth-century artists, such as Masaccio and Uccello, who responded to classical and naturalistic influences, and those more *retardataire* artists such as Fra Angelico and Benozzo Gozzoli, and certain later Umbrian painters such as Perugino, whose inspiration he deemed to be strongly Christian. This concept implied the rejection of an entire tradition, based on ideals of naturalism and beauty, going back to antiquity and codified in academic theory from the Renaissance onwards. It was under this influence that almost an entire generation of British writers travelled through Italy, most notably Lord Lindsay, James Dennistoun,[3] and John Ruskin.

The place and moment of Lindsay's conversion can be pinpointed with precision: he was on the road from Rome to Assisi travelling with his cousins James and Anne when he first picked up Rio's book, and its impact on his aesthetic responses was instantaneous. On 20 May 1839, having just reached Assisi, Lindsay recorded in his journal how they had:

'halted at S. Maria degli Angeli, and after visiting the church built over the house where St. Francis received his first call, and admiring a beautiful fresco of Overbeke's, quite in the spirit of the école mystique, drove up to Assisi, the picturesque old convent of the Franciscans, and peculiarly interesting in the history of art as the cradle of that pure and religious school of painting, which beginning with Giotto, and carried on by Fra Angelico, Benedetto Gozzoli and Perugino, found its highest development in Raphael.'

The journey home took Lindsay to Munich. Already fired up by Rio, he was quite unprepared for the impact of King Ludwig of Bavaria's recent efforts to propagate a new national art. Peter Cornelius had been brought to the city in 1819 to decorate the Glyptothek and had been occupied from 1830 onwards in a vain attempt to vie with Signorelli and Michelangelo in interpreting the *Creation and Last Judgement* in the Ludwigskirche. Meanwhile, in 1827, Julius Schnorr von Carolsfeld had followed Cornelius to Munich, where King Ludwig had hired him to decorate part of the Residenz with scenes from the Nibelungen Saga. 'I at least have been quite taken by surprise', Lindsay confessed in his travel journal:

'I had heard and read indeed that Munich, a place till the last thirty years utterly void of interest, was becoming, under King Louis' auspices, one of the most remarkable towns in Europe, but I always thought the accounts exaggerated ... Art I fancied (in its higher departments, I mean - fresco, religious painting etc.) was extinct for ever – gladly, gladly do I find myself mistaken.'

Lindsay admired above all the frescoes by Heinrich Maria von Hess in the Aller Heiliger, preferring their qualities of 'tenderness, purity and holiness' to the 'grandeur and severity' of Cornelius's *Last Judgement*, or even to 'the Gothic spirit of chivalry' which he had enjoyed in Schnorr's *Nibelungen Lied*. Hess, he concluded, 'has evidently drunk deeply of the spirit of the old Christian painters and retaining all that was excellent, avoided all that was mistaken in their notions - those of the times they lived in'.

By Christmas 1839 he had started to devise a complicated 'scheme of the poetry and prose of painting' which he expounded in a letter to James on New Year's Eve. Lindsay's basic idea, clearly inspired by further reflection on *De La*

Poésie Chrétienne, was that 'precedence in art, or in literature ... is to be regulated by the moral elevation of the artist, by the nobler or more degraded aspect in which he views the works of God, and by the degree in which his influence is a blessing to his fellow creatures or the reverse'. It was at this moment in Lindsay's personal development that he at last found sufficient confidence to resist, with absolute finality, persistent parental pressures to stand for election to Parliament. 'The cultivation of the intellect requires a private life', he confided to Anne (letter of 23 January 1840), and he went on to outline his personal ambitions in the intellectual field: '... I have many schemes, grand noble schemes, floating before me, and which, please God to spare me, I hope to fix and realise - the providential history of Man (which I told you I planned at Thebes sitting on the broken obelisk), a Poem (I feel it in me, dear Anne) ... a work on Art to lead men to the true moral and religious dignity and object ... and another on Love, that of God to Man, as provocative of love to God and to our neighbour.'

It was in this speculative frame of mind that Lindsay set off once more for Italy in 1840. He had been invited to stay with James and Anne at their rented home in Florence, the Villa Torregiani. They generally avoided the fashionable English community, Anne preferring her regular visits to the church of the Carmine, where she was making reduced copies of the Masaccio frescoes. There were regular visits from Félicie de Fauveau, the French sculptor, who, as a fervent royalist, had been living as an exile in Florence since 1836, and who was then making a bust portrait of Anne. Félicie de Fauveau was of particular interest to the Lindsays as a friend and admirer of Rio; indeed it was her copy of *De La Poésie Chrétienne* which James and Anne had lent to Lord Lindsay outside Assisi in 1839. And it was under her firm control that the Lindsays included visits to Siena and San Gimignano among their holiday excursions. These are vividly evoked by Lord Lindsay in a letter to a friend in Scotland (Robertson Glasgow) dated 13 June 1840:

'James, Anne and I made two or three very interesting excursions into Tuscany - the first to Pistoia, Lucca ... and Pisa, the second to the three convents of Vallombrosa, Camaldoli, and La Verna, Arezzo and Siena, San Gimignano, Volterra and so home. You must know that we have all three become passionate lovers of the ancient Italian painters - the contemporaries of Dante, Petrarch and Boccaccio, who revived the art and dedicated their efforts to the noblest end, the propagation of Christian truth and principle among the people - an end which in proportion as paganism and the classics became the favourite intellectual food of Europe, to the exclusion of the Bible, sank more and more into disrepute, till at last mere anatomical accuracy, colouring, drawing, etc., in short the mere mechanism of the art came to be considered the great desideratum, to the comparative neglect of the poetry and feeling of the subject represented, which if a sacred one, must of course be a failure if the heart do not inspire the hand.'[4]

At the end of the summer Lindsay returned to Haigh, armed with engravings after Fra Angelico and a copy of Raphael's *Madonna del Cardellino* in the Uffizi. He was accompanied by his sixteen year-old cousin, Coutts, who was to be his guest and pupil. He was now preoccupied by the necessity of finding a promising young English artist to whom he might address his book on Christian art. Coutts's physical proximity, as much as his burgeoning talents, may account for the extraordinary letter on the subject which Lindsay addressed to Anne on 10 December 1840:

'Dear Anne, here we are striving to revive the spirit of the past and restore the Arts to a sense of their due vocation, but where in England shall I find the man to follow up my views, who will be my disciple? Who will set the example! For artists, poor devils, must follow the fashion and pander to the bad taste of the time till a better spirit is breathed into it - they must paint to live before they can live to paint. I want a man independent in every sense of the term. Why Coutts is the man! give him only fair opportunities, enable him to acquire mastery over the mechanism of the art both in oils and fresco, store his mind well, and with the knowledge of human nature he will acquire in active life, and the inspiration of his own noble and Christianized heart within, with his singular talent of observation and his equanimity (to return united with genius) I see no earthly reason why he should not be a second Benozzo Gozzoli - aye, or rival to anyone whose name we may rank still higher in the scale of excellence. And it would be a glorious vocation ...'.

A year later Lindsay returned to Italy to make notes for his book, accompanied by his younger brother, Colin, and his new protegé, Coutts. He had just read Luigi Lanzi's *Storia Pittorica della Italia* (1795), with its emphasis on the strong independent tradition of local schools of painting, and appreciated the need to broaden his own approach. They arrived in Rome in December 1841 and Lindsay, doubtless anxious for some independence, lost no time before engaging tutors for the boys in his charge. Johann Wittmer, a pupil of Cornelius and the son-in-law of Koch, was hired as a drawing master for Coutts. His style, Lindsay assured a friend of the boy's mother, 'somewhat resembles Fra Angelico's'.[5]

Wittmer was also commissioned to make copies of what Lindsay describes as:

'a most beautiful series of Byzantine compositions embroidered (from celebrated paintings on mosaic probably of the time) on the Dalmatica or robe with which St Leo invested Charlemagne at his Coronation ... it was worked at Constantinople, and gives one a very high degree of the Greek art at that time'. Later he discovered that this celebrated sacerdotal robe in the Vatican dates from as late as the twelfth or thirteenth century; and although this new knowledge did not in any way weaken his belief in the artistic superiority of Eastern over Western art in the ninth and tenth centuries, it did reinforce his equally firm conviction of the quality of the Byzantine revival under the Comneni. Lindsay's interest in the Dalmatica is but one of many instances of his appreciation of the importance and quality of Byzantine art, which he believed had been seriously underestimated, even by those who had responded to the rising taste for Italian Primitives.

In general, however, Lindsay's comments on individual works of art throughout the 1842 tour are notable neither for their originality nor their critical penetration. He appears to have had no eye for detail, no capacity for connoisseurship or even for more generalised stylistic criticism; and his tendency towards abstraction and moral censure, inherited initially from Rio, was still pervasive. Moreover, the speed at which he journeyed through the Italian peninsula from Naples to Venice, mainly visiting pre-selected sites described in his guidebooks, itself inhibited unscheduled digressions which might have led to independent discoveries.[6]

At Assisi the tempo slackened long enough to enable Lindsay to compile detailed notes on 'every individual fresco that could in any way be of interest with reference to early art'. He was interested principally in questions of iconography, guided by De Natalibus's *Lives of the Saints*, a fifteenth-century volume outlining 'all the legends in their unadorned simplicity', which he had bought in Rome and now carried every-

where. His task was facilitated by his fortunate acquisition in Assisi of a series of reproductive drawings of every fresco in the upper and lower church, executed from scaffolding some thirty years earlier by G.B. Mariani. Not unreasonably, Lindsay had decided that the revolutionary quality of Giotto's frescoes lay in the fact that the artist had been 'obliged to create a new style in order to delineate feelings and sentiments unthought of, at least as yet unexpressed by the Greeks – to reflect in short the new spirit which had entered into the heart of the people.' Indeed, it was on the strength of the 'originality and expressive' power of the St Francis cycle in the upper church that Lindsay became convinced by Vasari's attribution of the frescoes to Giotto, a view which had been questioned by some nineteenth-century writers, including Von Rumohr. Lindsay did, however, disagree with Vasari's view that Cimabue rather than Giotto should be credited with the revival of painting in Italy. For Lindsay, only the Sienese school of Mino and Duccio took precedence over Giotto, and even this view was soon to be revised after he had seen the Giotto frescoes at the Arena Chapel in Padua and those of his followers, Altichiero and Giusto de' Menabuoi, in the same city. For by the time he wrote his book, Lindsay had concluded that the 'dramatic principle' of Giottesque art 'must necessarily take the lead' before the 'contemplative' style of Siena could 'do itself justice'.

It was thanks to Lindsay's increasing reliance on Vasari as his principal source that he found himself in front of Piero della Francesca's frescoes in San Francesco, Arezzo. For although Vasari described them in some detail, they had been virtually ignored by most later writers, with the notable exception of Lanzi. When Lindsay found them, they were in distressing condition, 'absolutely in the last agonies of dissolution, hanging in flakes from the walls'. Yet he could still perceive their quality, not only the artist's mastery of perspective, but also the dramatic sense of movement – 'in the procession you feel the march of a vast multitude' – combined with the classical quality of 'graceful ease and repose which we have lost since the 16th century'. Coutts, too, is reported as having compared the integrated compositions of these monumental frescoes with the Elgin Marbles. This, ostensibly at least, was the major discovery of Lindsay's tour and one that apparently stimulated uncharacteristic visual responses as opposed to mere moral approbation. Or could it have been the precocious young Coutts, rather than his more voluble mentor, who had first responded to the spirit of the Antique evoked by Piero's art?

Good Friday marked the departure of Coutts from Italy. He was due to enlist in the Guards, but Lindsay still nursed higher ambitions for him. Then, one day in April, Lindsay walked into Molini's shop in Florence and found the English language edition of Franz Kugler's *Handbook of the History of Painting,* edited by Charles Eastlake and published in 1842. Naturally, his first concern was to discover to what extent the German writer might have trodden on the ground he had marked out for his own book. But, although he acknowledged the quality of Kugler's connoisseurship, Lindsay was reassured that the necessity for his own work was in no way diminished. For while Kugler's work, unlike most other books on early Italian art, had the advantage of being published in English, it lacked popular appeal and would not, Lindsay felt, attract 'the uninitiated pure spirited youthful English aristocracy for whom I write'. He then went on to characterise it, somewhat disparagingly, as 'flowing on a continuous stream of criticism, unrelieved by break or rapid, anecdote or biography, criticism, criticism, criticism to the end'. By this he meant of course detailed stylistic analysis, a visual emphasis conspicuously lacking from his own art historical and critical vocabulary.

Then, almost feverishly, Lindsay set about preparing a detailed scheme for his own contribution. From his long letter to Anne of 7 May 1842, it becomes evident that his principal motivating idea was still more or less the same as the one he had outlined to James in 1839, but fortified now by a belief, which he had not hitherto expressed in such singularly nationalistic terms, that 'Providence, in committing the pure faith to the custody of England and placing her on the throne of the civilized world, enjoins her to carry the spirit of Christianity into every department of genius, every walk of life'. This remark reflects the beginning of a new preoccupation that was to haunt him more and more during the next five years: that the religious outlook of his mentor, Rio, while 'admirable for the French and Roman Catholics' was 'forgive me, rather narrow bottomed' and dogmatic.

Finally, Lindsay assured Anne that, in spite of possible indications to the contrary, he did not contemplate a work 'like Agincourt's or Cicognara's of six or seven volumes and a thumping folio of plates'.7 On the contrary, he had in mind no more than a modest series of letters to a young artist or friend just gone out to Italy. This unusual form would, he hoped, free him from the responsibility of a professed historian, while leaving him scope to 'offer a thousand hints, conjecture etc. in an offhand way – to blend with criticism, description, anecdote, reminiscence, allusion ad infinitum – in short to range at freedom through the pleasant fields of fresco, roaring and lashing my tail ad libitum'.

It is from Lindsay's account of his visit to Modena (letter of 3 June 1842) that we can perhaps most readily conjure an image of this shy, solitary but humorous and self-deprecating scholar making his relentless progress from Florence across Northern Italy to complete his tour:

'You would be amused, dear Anne, seeing me on my explorations – the laquais perhaps following me ... with the large folio De Natalibus under his arm ... as for being stared at I have long grown callous to it – the other day while making my notes on the sculptures outside the Cathedral at Modena I had about twenty people round me; sometimes the priests come to see what I am about – I always make a civil observation and then take no further notice of them, and they generally soon go. The people take me for a queer fish, I fancy, but I don't care for that. The ciceronis too don't know what to make of me – I have regularly to break them in; it takes about an hour to do so generally a quick curt yet courteous manner answers my purpose admirably, and I never allow myself to be diverted from my object. As for the custodes, they get terribly weary, cough, or rattle their keys, all to no purpose – I remain quite callous till they sit down in despair or resignation. Sometimes rather ludicrous incidents happen. The other day, intensely occupied with a picture in the choir of a church, I advanced into the middle of it; whether or not the stalls were filled with the canons before I entered, or whether they took their place while I was standing there in a state of abstraction, I know not, but you may imagine the start it gave me, the whole assembly suddenly bursting out in full chant, within ten feet of me – believing myself alone. And I did not even blush. In short pro tempore my character seems totally changed, and I have become one of the most confident, self possessed, determined men of action in Europe.'

Home again at Haigh at the end of August, Lindsay addressed himself to the final form of his book on Christian art. James and Anne were in Florence and spent the Christmas holiday discussing with their old friend Félicie de Fauveau the 'General Classification of Schools and Artists' which Lindsay had devised for his book. On 28 December 1842 Anne duly reported back to Lindsay with a summary of Félicie's criticisms and ideas. But Lindsay made it clear that he had no wish to continue a dialogue with De Fauveau on the subject of Italian art. It was a question of his religious beliefs, and of a 'consciousness that I differ from her views as a Roman Catholic so decidedly on many points, while I go along with her in others so far beyond the limits of Protestants, that I find myself constantly awkwardly situated ... with her'. Or, as he expressed it again a little later, 'How could I explain or reconcile the delight I take in some of the Legends of the Saints and the scorn with which I regard others – how without apparent obstinacy and real insincerity maintain views in conversation which on her principles are wrong but on mine true? I felt in a degree the same embarrassment that a Puseyite must be sensible of in conversing with a Catholic ...'.

Anne, however, was not readily appeased by Lindsay's excuses, especially when, in February 1843, she discovered that Rio was at that very moment filling his notebooks in exemplary fashion with De Fauveau's ideas and information, for use in a forthcoming supplementary volume to *De la Poésie Chrétienne*. Yet her uncharacteristically tactless and ill-judged letter on this matter, with fascinating gossip about Rio's friendship with the leaders of the Oxford Movement in England, can only have aggravated Lindsay's acute anxiety and strengthened his determination to prune his aesthetic ideas of any associations that might be construed as Roman Catholic or Puseyite:

'We have had a very pleasant visitor at Florence lately – but who I am afraid if you do not make the better haste may forestall you in many of your observations', she wrote. 'I mean Rio who with his family is travelling in Italy picking up materials for another volume. We have seen him very often and there is much to like in him. I never saw a Frenchman do such ample justice to the English character – he speaks English as well as you do – he has written but not yet published a work on the influence of Catholicism (Roman) on art in England – particularly relating to Architecture ... It is curious to hear him speak of puseyism and of his expectations from it. He has seen and conversed with many of the leaders of the party and they seem to have been much more open in their admissions to him than they are to the public. He leaves this next Saturday for Rome. Having travelled thro' all Germany, Dresden, Vienna etc to Venice where he passed some weeks in pursuit of his object. Here his great object seems to be to *suck the brains of* Mademoiselle de Fauveau who surprises me more & more by her original views and the great mass of information she possesses. I cannot tell you how angry both James and I have often felt at you for not making more use of her. I really think you were very foolish and as to your reason about catholic views, I cannot see that it was one at all, for you were not bound to her opinions but might receive them and modify them as best pleased you. She said to me more than once I am sorry Lord Lindsay did not come oftener to see me. I would much have preferred giving him any little knowledge I possessed than giving it to Rio – but he apparently did not wish for it. Perhaps she was right. At any rate I feel so savage with you at this moment that it is lucky for you you are not here so that you escape a predestinate scratched face ... One thing comforts me about Rio – he is going to lose his time and throw away his power in analysing and attacking the bad schools and proving that they ought not to be admired, for which purpose he visits every object in the decadence of art and criticises it. Now this will tire people, he had better show what is worthy of admiration and having given people a good taste the bad will fail by itself. His great hobby horse at present is the downfall of Michael Angelo – but he will break his horns against that Rock if he does not take care. He is full of Eloquence and enthusiams and will talk by the hour and excite himself so that he cannot sleep all night. His taste appears to me incorrect or rather so full of prepossession that he will go into raptures at any daub of the early times and can find no beauty in the best pictures painted after a certain date – it is amusing to see Félicie check his extasies and say – ne regardez pas cela il n'y a pas grand' chose – on which he quietly withdraws – and begins to apostrophise another picture. Nevertheless he will write well and I should greatly wish you to be before hand with him. A part of his plan is to embody his ideas in a sort of tale. He will present an individual entering into life with the warmest admiration for all classical art and learning, travelling in Italy with these feelings and with great contempt for the religious school of art. Some great event happens in his life, Rio did not tell me what, which entirely changes his feelings, gives him another turn of mind and his second tour in Italy is described with all his new impressions and new delights. I think this may be a very bright notion if well worked out. His first object in entering a town is to get together all the legends and stories of saints, patriots etc and to make himself well acquainted with them so as to put himself as much as possible in sympathy with the painting. In this he does much as you do – but he intends writing his work in Italy that he may not get cold – great part of it he says at Venice where he has a great many followers and admirers – it is rather drôle to hear him talk of "Mon Ecole". He is a good specimen of a Frenchman but a Frenchman still.'[8]

Lindsay did not share Rio's current 'hobby horse', the 'downfall of Michelangelo'. For he considered Michelangelo to have been almost 'protestant in reason' and in his recognition of our Saviour as the prime object of worship, even if he remained Catholic 'in heart and imagination'. 'I have not yet in every particular made up my mind about Michelangelo', he conceded in a letter from Haigh of 28 February 1843, 'and I fully admit that his was a deviation from the line of traditional Christian art; still, though bad at a Madonna he is profoundly lofty and religious in his *spirit*; his Holy Family in the Tribune I will not stand for, but the Sistine Chapel was the last grand protest of Christianity against Paganism South of the Alps, the dying blast or rather echo of Savonarola's trumpet, like Roland's at Fontarabia, the last and loudest, prophetic and full of woe.'

By February 1846 Lindsay had completed his manuscript. It amounted to an introductory essay on Christian iconography, followed by the 'General Classification of Schools and Artists'; and then ten essays or letters on Roman art; Byzantine art; Lombard and Gothic architecture; sculpture of the Lombards and the Italo-Byzantine revivals; Nicola Pisano; Giotto and his school; the school of Siena; the semi-Byzantine succession at Florence – Orcagna and Fra Angelico; the primitive school of Bologna; and finally sculpture and painting North of the Alps. Having followed Lindsay on his tours through Italy, we find little to surprise us in the strictly art-historical passages of the book, although the depth and range of his literary sources is impressive. He frequently turns to Lorenzo Ghiberti's *Commentarii* (begun c.1447) in his discussion of Giotto and his followers; and he relies heavily on Guglielmo della Valle's compilation of documents, *Lettere Senesi* (1782–6), in his account of the Sienese school. On the other hand, the well-researched iconographical section at the very beginning does require further comment. The vogue for medieval hagiography probably began

with Rio's friend the Comte de Montalembert, best known for his volume of essays *Du Vandalisme et du Catholicisme dans l'art* (1839). It was continued in France by Adolphe-Napoléon Didron (1806–67), who in a far more scholarly manner investigated the sources, symbols and meaning of Byzantine and Western medieval art and published the *Histoire de Dieu* in 1845. His principal sources were the Bible, *The Golden Legend*, and the twelfth and thirteenth-century *Historia Scolastica*, *Bible historiée* and *Speculum Universalis*. Although Lindsay frequently acknowledges Didron, especially in his chapters on Byzantine art, his own interest in the subject had been developed independently during his travels and his preferred reference book, as we have noted, was the *Catalogus Sanctorum* of Petrus de Natalibus, a Venetian compilation made at the end of the fourteenth century and printed in 1493. Lindsay was fully conscious of the origins of some of these visual traditions in the legends of the Eastern world, but it is nevertheless disconcerting to find this section of the book headed *Christian Mythology, Legends of Saints...* . The explanation for Lindsay's deliberate use of this provocative term undoubtedly lies in his determination not to be mistaken either for a Roman Catholic who actually believed in all the medieval legends and devotional practices associated with them, or even for another Mrs Jameson, the popular author of a series of articles on *Sacred and Legendary Art*, whose aim, in his opinion, was to 'give the legends in the most romantic and sentimental manner'. He wished to applaud the pure religious spirit of the early Italian artists but, as a Protestant, he could not associate himself unreservedly with their far from rational religious faith, and as an arbiter of artistic merit he could not entirely overlook their technical limitations and imperfections. Nor could he bring himself to dismiss all pagan and classic art simply on the grounds that it expressed a humanist and unchristian philosophy. 'Do not for a moment suppose me insensible to Classic Art', he reminds his readers, for 'the memories of Greece and of the Palatine are very dear to me – I cannot speak coldly of the Elgin marbles, or the Apollo, the Venus, the Dying Gladiator, the Niobe, the Diana of Gabii, the Psyche of Naples...'. It was to resolve this internal conflict that he devised a determinist philosophy of historical evolution by which man progressively advances towards the truth by a dialectical process resulting from the antagonism of half-truths. This concept enabled Lindsay to take refuge in the dynamic ideal of a second regeneration of Catholic (in the sense of universal) Christianity, which he hoped might be realised within his own lifetime. Such regeneration would be a conscious and deliberate gesture, and Lindsay's book on Christian art was designed to prompt some independent English artist to set the process in motion by the example of his vision.

Lindsay's narrow, determinist view of historical and artistic evolution may have succeeded in clearing him of any suspicion of harbouring Roman Catholic or Puseyite sympathies, but it provoked the wrath of his two principal reviewers, John Ruskin and Nicholas Wiseman who, three years later, was to be appointed Cardinal Archbishop of Westminster. Ruskin complained wittily in the *Quarterly Review* of Lindsay's 'triplicity',[9] while Wiseman expressed angry distaste for Lindsay's 'irreverent eyes' and 'flippant tongue'.[10]

There is, alas, no record of Coutts Lindsay's reaction. As for the central creative role he had been invited to assume, so as to give fresh impetus to the progression of Christian art, it remained unfulfilled. The future for Coutts lay elsewhere: in his exclusive Grosvenor Gallery, in the neo-pagan values of the aesthetic movement, and, of course, in the inevitable association with Gilbert and Sullivan's Bunthorne, a 'greenery yallery Grosvenor Gallery Foot-in-the-grave young man'.

NOTES AND REFERENCES

This study is based on the private papers of Lord Lindsay, most of which were formerly deposited at the John Rylands University Library in Manchester and are currently on deposit at the National Library of Scotland, Edinburgh. My two essays for this catalogue are revised and greatly shortened versions of two articles published in the *Bulletin of the John Rylands University Library of Manchester*, vol.64, no.1, Autumn 1981, pp.27–60 and vol.64 no.2, Spring 1982, pp.287–333. During my research at that time I received valuable advice and warm encouragement from Professor Francis Haskell, and when I last saw him at a dinner party in Oxford he had been looking forward with characteristic enthusiasm to this exhibition. I would like to dedicate my contributions to the catalogue to his memory.

1. F. Haskell, 'Gibbon and the History of Art' in *Past and Present in Art and Taste. Selected Essays*, New Haven and London, 1987, pp.16–29.

2. For a general discussion of all these issues see G. Previtali, 'La Fortuna dei primitivi dal Vasari ai Neoclassici', Turin, 1964; and A. Chastel 'Le Goût des Préraphaëlites en France' in *De Giotto à Bellini*, exhibition catalogue, Paris, Orangerie, 1956.

3. For Dennistoun's book, his views on Rio and his friendship with Lord Lindsay, see H. Brigstocke 'Memoirs of the Dukes of Urbino' in *I Della Rovere nell' Italia delle Corti*, Atti del Convegno, Urbania, 1999 (in press).

4. A copy of this letter is preserved among Lord Lindsay's papers. The original has not been traced.

5. Letter to Miss Jean Trotter, Rome, 9 December 1841. Jean Trotter was the sister of Anne Lindsay's father, and was, therefore, related to Lord Lindsay by his marriage to Margaret Lindsay.

6. Lindsay's notebooks from this tour have apparently not survived. We can, nevertheless, follow the progress of his travels in detail from the long and carefully composed letters he sent home to Anne. All quotations relating to the journey from Rome to Florence are taken from a letter dated Florence, Easter Monday, 28 March 1842.

7. L. Cicognara, *Storia della Scultura*, Venice, 1813–18. Lindsay is probably referring to the second edition of 1820. For the impact of Gibbon on this great historian of Italian sculpture, see F. Haskell 'Cicognara eretico' in *Giuseppe Jappelli e il suo tempo*, edited by G. Mazzi, Padua, 1982.

8. Letter to Lord Lindsay dated Florence, 16 February 1843. For further thoughts on Rio, see R. Lightbown 'The Inspiration of Christian Art' in *Influences in Victorian Art and Architecture*, edited by S. Macready and F. Thompson (Occasional Paper VII of the Society of Antiquaries of London), London, 1985.

9. *Quarterly Review*, June 1847, pp.1–57. For Ruskin the difference between Christian and Pagan art was not a question of dialectics but an unbridgeable gulf. 'The separation is not gradual, but instant and final – the difference not of degree, but of condition; it is the difference between the dead vapours rising from a stagnant pool, and the same vapours touched by a torch.' See further J. Steegman, *Consort of Taste*, London, 1950, pp.70–3.

10. For Wiseman's review, written jointly with John Steinmetz, see the *Dublin Review*, July 1836, pp.435–60.

Lord Lindsay as a Collector of Paintings

HUGH BRIGSTOCKE

We have seen how a proper appreciation of Lord Lindsay's *Sketches of the History of Christian Art* depends on an understanding of the extent to which he regarded his book as an illustration of his all-embracing determinist philosophy of history. His attitude to collecting from the 1840s until the mid-1870s must also be considered in a wider context. His ambition was to form a private museum and library which would represent all branches of science, literature and art, and all stages in the development of the human intellect. As he himself was to record nostalgically in 1865: 'I had, in fact, in my earliest youth determined to assemble together the wisest and most graceful thinkers of all countries, ages, and pursuits, as agreeable companions, instructive teachers, and honoured guests, under the symbolical pavilion of the Lindsays, who, with their friends, might thus converse hereafter, as in the School of Athens, with congenial associates in whatever branches of literature, art, or science, their genius or taste should severally direct them to.'[1]

We should not, therefore, expect to find Lindsay's picture collection limited to the works of the fourteenth-century masters about whom he had written so eloquently in 1847. Yet it still comes as a considerable surprise to discover that between the late 1850s and the early 1870s he extended his range sufficiently to acquire works attributed to Bolognese *seicento* artists such as Annibale Carracci and Guido Reni, and even a Dutch animal painting attributed to Paulus Potter. For these were precisely the categories of painting which he had most vehemently con-

demned in the 1840s after reading Rio's *De La Poésie Chrétienne*.

It was in 1833, when he was still only twenty-one, that Lindsay was able to take the first steps towards making his early dream a reality, after he had unexpectedly received a substantial legacy from a fairly distant relation, Lady Mary Crawford, who had been attracted by his enthusiasm for the family history. At first he concentrated on accumulating books, including incunabula, and it was only after his long European tour of 1842 that he began to make a serious attempt to build up a collection of pictures. His acquisitions before then were picked up in a seemingly casual manner during his wanderings abroad. In 1840, for instance, he had bought in Florence a copy of Raphael's *Madonna del Cardellino*, and had also commissioned a Florentine painter named Marini to draw him copies of some of Benozzo Gozzoli's frescoes in San Gimignano. Two years later Marini had also made him a copy of the head of Dante from the newly uncovered Giottesque frescoes in the Bargello in Florence. A little earlier the same year, while he was in Rome with his cousin Coutts, Lindsay had commissioned a copy of the *Dalmatica di San Leone*, a sacerdotal vestment in the Vatican, and had also bought two fine early Italian paintings, a fourteenth-century Florentine *Crucifixion* now attributed to Giovanni da Milano (cat.no.5), and a *Sts Agatha and Lucy* by Matteo di Giovanni (cat.no.21).

However, it was only after Lindsay returned from these travels and heard that the celebrated *Last Judgement* attributed to Fra Angelico in the collection of Cardinal Fesch in Rome (fig.8) might be for sale, that the full extent of his ambitions as a picture collector became apparent. He had first admired the Fra Angelico in 1829 and now listed it as a major desideratum for his museum, idly boasting to Anne: 'I would ... pledge myself to write the Life and Panegyric of Adam Smith sooner than not possess it.'[2] Yet when the moment came to make an offer, he instructed a friend in Rome who had been making enquiries on his behalf to limit herself to a mere £150, or at the very most £200, which was quickly rejected.[3]

After this early setback, Lindsay elected to make a more modest but more decisive beginning, and in April 1843 he commissioned a full-size copy of Perugino's *Christ on the Mount of Olives* (now in the Palazzo Pitti) from the Florentine artist Vicenzo Corsi (active 1843 – after 1877), at a fee of £75. James, who was staying in Florence at this time, had already told Lindsay of Corsi's proficiency and had himself just bought from

Fig.8 · Attributed to Fra Angelico (c.1395–1455)
The Last Judgement
Gemäldegalerie, Berlin

Fig.9 · Vicenzo Corsi (active 1843–after 1877)
The Adoration of the Magi (after Gentile da Fabriano)
The Parish of St Paul the Apostle, Croxteth, Liverpool

him a copy of Perugino's *Entombment* in the Uffizi.[4] These two acquisitions marked the beginning of long association with the Florentine painter, and there followed a succession of valuable commissions from Lindsay for full-scale replicas of other major works of art in the Florentine museums and churches. They included Raphael's *Vision of Ezekiel* (Palazzo Pitti) in 1843; Lorenzo di Credi's *Nativity* (Accademia) in 1845; selected details from the Masaccio and Filippino Lippi frescoes in the Brancacci Chapel in the church of the Carmine;[5] Ridolfo Ghirlandaio's *St Zenobius Raising a Child* (Accademia), in 1848; Fra Angelico's *Coronation of the Virgin* (Uffizi) in 1849; Gentile da Fabriano's *Adoration of the Magi* (Uffizi; fig.9) and Fra Angelico's *Santa Trinita Deposition* (San Marco) in 1867;[6] Carlo Dolci's *Poesia* (then in the Corsini Gallery); and Andrea del Sarto's *Cenacolo di San Salvi* in 1877. Lindsay had no doubts as to the utility of these large-scale replicas, and on 7 June 1848 assured his mother, with particular reference to the copies after Masaccio, that they 'will be *invaluable* hereafter, and even in our own times, for the frescoes have never been copied in large … and may create new artists as of old they created Leonardo da Vinci and Raphael'. Evidently he had not abandoned the idea, voiced a year earlier in the *Sketches of the History of Christian Art*, that contemporary British artists might be inspired by study of Italian Old Masters to create a new modern style of religious painting.

During the years 1843–6, when he was mainly living at home and writing his *Sketches of the History of Christian Art*, Lindsay apparently made little effort to acquire, either at home or abroad, original works of art to supplement the copies he was ordering from Corsi, in spite of the fact that his father had just bought him an estate at Echt in Aberdeenshire, at a cost of around £150,000. In June 1846 Lindsay became engaged to his cousin Margaret (Min) and they were married at St George's, Hanover Square, London. In November he bought a vast picture of *Moses on Mount Sinai* by Benjamin West, measuring 18 × 12 feet (about 5.5 × 3.7 metres), for which he paid 200 guineas, and which is now in Westminster Hall in the Houses of Parliament. He had ignored the advice of his cousin Coutts, who had made the alternative suggestion that, as a 'noble experiment', he might employ George Richmond to paint a fresco. However, to judge from the letter he wrote to Anne on 28 November 1846, Lindsay soon appears to have felt some regret for his lapse in taste: 'I have considered it all along as a furniture picture agreeable to the eye as regards colouring, light, etc. but not to be subjected to

the critical rules by which you would judge a work of high art.'

In 1847 the Lindsays went to Paris and then on to Florence, where Lindsay saw the Lombardi-Baldi collection of early Italian art, which had already attracted the attention of William Coningham, MP for Brighton, and his adviser, the dealer Samuel Woodburn. But like Coningham, who was one of the most discerning picture buyers in Britain in the mid-nineteenth century, Lindsay was disappointed to learn that the collection, which consisted of about a hundred early Italian pictures, including some dating from the thirteenth century, could only be bought *en bloc* for a sum approaching £12,000. This precluded any negotiations on his part, even if he did tell his mother (7 June 1848) that he would have been prepared to part with as much as £3,500 for thirty unspecified items of his own choice.

Admitting defeat, he resolved to refer the matter to the Commissioners of the National Gallery in London. Eventually, in 1857, after fifteen years of virtual paralysis as a buying institution and following a Parliamentary enquiry into its acquisition policy, the Gallery succeeded in purchasing twenty-two major works of art from the Lombardi-Baldi collection, including a vast altarpiece of the *Coronation of the Virgin* in the style of Orcagna, for around £7,000. By then Sir Charles Eastlake was Director and, with the help of Otto Mündler, the Gallery's German agent on the Continent, was buying aggressively to establish a more art-historically oriented collection.

After returning to Britain in 1848, Lindsay appears to have shown no further interest in buying pictures until the Thomas Blayds sale, which took place at Christie's on 30 and 31 March 1849. It was at this little-publicised auction of a somewhat mediocre, but not uninteresting, collection that he first really took the plunge as a picture collector, buying twenty-six lots for a modest outlay of just under £200. Among his more successful acquisitions must be counted a series of four predella panels now attributed to Luca di Tommè (cat.no.4), but then offered under an attribution to Giotto, which Lindsay apparently accepted. He also bought two predella panels by Signorelli representing *Scenes from the Lives of Sts Joachim and Anne* and *The Birth of the Virgin* (cat.no.24), a *Meeting of Jephthah and his Daughter* sold under the name of Orcagna but now tentatively attributed to Benvenuto di Giovanni (cat.no.22), and a *Madonna and Child* sold as a Vivarini and catalogued here under Tuscan School (cat.no.13). He also bid successfully for a number of cassone panels, including a pair representing the story of Solomon and the Queen of Sheba now attributed to Scheggia (cat.no.10). Yet he failed to secure one of the best lots in the sale, consisting of three fragments from a dismembered polyptych by Simone Martini (now in the Fitzwilliam Museum, Cambridge, fig.10), which fetched only £15 after the sale. The purchaser was the Revd John Fuller Russell of Eagle House, near Enfield, a high church Anglican who, as an undergraduate at Cambridge, had formed a close friendship with Pusey and became interested in the Oxford Movement.[7]

From his correspondence with Coutts, it appears that Lindsay approached the Blayds sale in the spirit of a bargain hunter, with no intention of limiting himself to works of major art-historical interest, or even to works by those early Italian painters who might have qualified for inclusion in Rio's *école mystique*. Indeed James, now Lindsay's father-in-law, who had hitherto always encouraged him in his academic researches on Italian art, understandably chose this moment to issue him with a word of warning against squandering his money by collecting in such an indiscriminate manner. 'I can go quite the length of understanding your wish for *specimens* of schools, or of old masters, but to fill your room with a heap of old Rubbish, I think you will one day regret', he wrote on 12 April 1848. And he continued: '... I would anxiously dissuade you from outlay which none but yourself and some very few others would appreciate and this only *for a short time*, because I feel the taste cannot last for *deformity* ... Some of these paintings are curious, some of them are good, but to possess a quantity of them would give one a distaste for painting generally.'

Yet this stern admonition does not appear to have deterred Lindsay, and a month later, at the Campe sale which took place in London on 13 May 1849, he was bidding in an equally opportunist manner for a picture of *Esther and Ahasuerus* attributed to Lucas van Leyden, an *Allegory of Melancholy* by Cranach (cat.no.29), and a *Virgin and Child*, now attributed to the Master of the Embroidered Foliage (cat.no.28), but then catalogued as a work of Dürer on the basis of a false signature. Together these three pictures cost £86. 2s. 0d.

However, the necessity of replying to his father-in-law's criticism stimulated Lindsay to define his aims as a collector with unusual precision in a long letter dated 22 April 1849:

'... The great object I set before me in early youth, when not more than seventeen or eighteen, and which I have kept steadily before me ever since, was to form a Museum – in the old Greek sense of the word – of specimens carefully selected so as to illustrate the respective works of Nature and Art, thus to educate not only my own mind, but that of our family generally, by creating a centre of intellectual and moral influence which should radiate to each member according as his innate disposition might render him predisposed and susceptible to this or that line of interest.

... In the first place, as you are well aware, the best works of the greatest masters are for the most part inaccessible to purchase, being either in churches or public galleries. Yet by these alone can the height and excellence of Art be known. I know what a prejudice exists against copies, and yet I do not think you will blame me when I avow that I prefer a good Copy of the best existing work of a great master to a second-rate or third-rate original – which is all, generally speaking, that is now attainable. Copies moreover are all that can be possibly obtained of some of the greatest masters, who worked almost entirely in fresco, for example Benozzo Gozzoli and Michael Angelo, – and many painters of whom original easel paintings may be obtained, are only to be truly estimated by their frescoes – Nay the greatest achievements of painting are in fresco. My plan therefore is to employ artists gifted with that peculiar genius which enters into, lives in, and reproduces, the ideas of others, without having any original conceptions of its own, to make accurate copies for me, the size of the originals, of some twenty of the most important frescoes of Italy, from Giotto to Leonardo, Raphael and M. Angelo – and also of the most important easel-paintings, Italian, Flemish, and German which form epochs in Art – limiting my purchase of original paintings to such as will fill up the gaps in the series so formed, and illustrate the progress and history of painting during the period contemplated. Of this class of paintings are those I have just purchased – of little interest or beauty in themselves, viewed as an entire collection, but which will link in and add their quota to the gallery which I thus propose to form. It is as such only I value them – as component parts of a great future whole, but, viewed at present in inevitable isolation, I do not wonder at your disesteem of them – while I believe notwithstanding that when that whole is completed you will feel differently ...'.

Lindsay's justification for putting the main emphasis of his picture collection on full-scale copies, on the grounds that first rate original works by the fifteenth- and sixteenth-century masters rarely came on to the market, was soon

Fig.10 · Simone Martini (c.1285–1344)
Sts Michael, Augustine and Ambrose
Fitzwilliam Museum, Cambridge

to be overtaken by events. For, less than two months later, on 9 June 1849, William Coningham's exceptionally well-chosen collection of pictures came up for sale at Christie's.[8] Among the outstanding Italian paintings offered were Antonello da Messina's *St Jerome* (fig.11), Mantegna's *The Agony in the Garden* (fig.12), Botticelli's *Adoration of the Kings*, Pollaiuolo's *Apollo and Daphne*, and Sebastiano del Piombo's *Madonna and Child with Saints*, all of which have since found their way into the National Gallery in London.

Although Lindsay viewed the sale and marked a catalogue, he apparently left no bids, thereby reinforcing the suspicion that he was still more interested in bargains (prices at the Coningham sale were relatively high) than in works of outstanding quality. Or perhaps he was temporarily short of funds. This was apparently the difficulty five years later, when an exceptionally beautiful *Crucifixion* attributed to Duccio (cat.no.2) fetched £278. 5s. 0d at the sale of E. Joly de Bammeville, a Frenchman who had been collecting early Italian art from the 1840s and who later converted to Roman Catholicism, following a visit to Oxford in 1851.[9] Lindsay was outbid by the Revd Walter Davenport-Bromley, Vicar of Fanshawe in Cheshire, another enthusiastic collector of early Italian art, who had bought well at the Fesch sale in Rome.[10] Both Charles Eastlake, acting in a private capacity, and the Prince Consort had also expressed interest in bidding for the Duccio and had been advised by Gladstone that there would be no conflict with the National Gallery.[11] All that Lindsay did manage to secure at this sale was

a group of miniatures attributed to Agnese Dolci, which fetched £17. 6s. 6d. (untraced). However, after the auction he also acquired a *Venus Reclining near a Fountain* by Cranach (fig.13), which, as lot 28, had fetched £15. 4s. 6d. On this same day, with a sudden switch of mood or taste, he successfully offered 50 guineas at the Henry Clayton Freeling sale for a *Landscape with Cattle* by Karel Dujardin (untraced).

Much of the credit for Lindsay's eventual achievement as a collector is due to William Spence, an English artist and dealer who was resident in Florence.[12] Lindsay probably first came into contact with him in 1856 while he and his family were staying at the Villino Borghese. Although Spence was at his best in the company of admiring ladies – even the usually level-headed Anne Lindsay conceded that he had 'a very pretty voice and sings beautifully'[13] – he could also be impressive in more serious company and certainly appreciated Lindsay's potential value as a client. Moreover Spence's stock was as versatile as his manner, and he was able to provide Lindsay and his wife with the maiolica and decorative furnishings they needed for their new home at Dunecht in Aberdeenshire (figs. 5 & 6) – Lindsay's father had given them £400 for this purpose – before tempting them with a selection of well-chosen pictures. In 1856 alone he sold them an early fifteenth-century Florentine painting, *The Intercession of Christ and the Virgin*, an iconographically unusual representation of the Trinity, which originally formed the main part of an altarpiece in the Duomo at Florence and now belongs to the Metropolitan Museum of Art,

New York (fig.14); an altarpiece of *The Virgin and Child Enthroned with St Francis, the Donor Agnoletta Benvenuti, the Archangel Raphael and Tobias*, then attributed to Cosimo Rosselli, but in fact by his contemporary Francesco Botticini (cat.no.19); a fifteenth-century panel, then attributed to Lorenzetti, showing the *Death of St Ephraim and other Scenes from the Lives of Hermits* (cat.no.11 or 12); a *St Barbara*, then attributed to Benozzo Gozzoli and now to Domenico Ghirlandaio (cat.no.15); a fine cabinet picture of *St John the Baptist*, then ascribed to the circle of Leonardo da Vinci and subsequently attributed to Cesare da Sesto and more recently to Bernardino Lanino (cat.no.30); and finally a small canvas connected with Tintoretto's celebrated picture of *The Body of St Mark Removed from the Funeral Pyre* (cat.no.34).

Two years later, in March 1858, Lindsay and his wife demonstrated the increasingly catholic range of their taste when they paid Mr Bruce, an Edinburgh picture restorer, £250 for a *Flight into Egypt* by Guido Reni, now owned by Bradford Art Galleries and Museums, which was probably brought to Britain from the Palazzo Colonna in Rome early in the nineteenth century (fig.15). Although the initiative in this case came from his wife, Lindsay, obviously happy to have an authentic specimen of Reni's style at a bargain price, readily acquiesced; while Min, spurred on by a rumour that the Royal Institution in Edinburgh was also considering the picture, settled the matter within the same week.

In August 1859 Lindsay laid out the surprisingly large sum of £836. 12s. od. on twelve pictures at the Northwick Park sale. It is probably fair to say that the money could have been spent better elsewhere. In June the following year, Samuel Woodburn's Masaccio *Madonna and Child* (now in the National Gallery) was sold at Christie's, as Gentile da Fabriano, for just 15 guineas; and in April 1861 Charles Eastlake bought Piero della Francesca's celebrated *Baptism of Christ* (also in the National Gallery) at the Uzielli sale for £241.10s. od. In the face of such alternatives, Lindsay's acquisitions at the Northwick Park sale are mainly of interest as further examples of his attempt to widen the range of his collection. The two best pictures he bought were a small *Holy Family*, which he believed to be by Ludovico Carracci, but which is now attributed to a follower of Simon Vouet, probably Nicolas Chaperon (fig.16); and a *Portrait of Philip Sydney*, then attributed to Antonis Mor and now thought to be by Moreelse. Curiously, he seems to have ignored the mystical Botticelli of *The Virgin Adoring the Sleeping Christ Child* recently acquired by the National Gallery of Scotland (fig.17), which was bought by Lord Elcho, later 10th Earl of Wemyss. As Wemyss later recorded in his private memoir, in language that could have been penned by Lindsay: 'Such is my admiration for the early Florentine school, so sublime in religious sentiment, so glorious in colour, so pure in design, that there is no Raphael for which I would give my Botticelli.'[14]

In June 1863 the Davenport-Bromley collection came on to the market, providing Lindsay with a second opportunity to secure the Duccio *Crucifixion* which he had lost at the De Bammeville sale. This time he was successful,

Fig.16 · Attributed to Nicolas Chaperon (1612–1654/5)
The Holy Family · Private Collection

Fig.17 · Sandro Botticelli (1444/5–1510)
The Virgin Adoring the Sleeping Christ Child
National Gallery of Scotland, Edinburgh

Fig.18 · Ugolino di Nerio (active 1317–died 1339/49)
Sts Bartholomew and Andrew · National Gallery, London

and had to pay only £262. 10s. 0d, some £15 less than it had cost its previous owner. He also bought, for six guineas, a panel of *Sts Bartholomew and Andrew* from a dismembered altarpiece by Ugolino di Nerio; it is now in the National Gallery, London (fig.18). But he ignored an important group of pictures that Davenport-Bromley had acquired from the Fesch collection. Perhaps it was as an antidote to the austerity of the Duccio that Lindsay then bought, in the same year, a Paulus Potter (£70 from Bruce of Edinburgh) and the *Head of an Apostle* by an artist close to Palma Vecchio, which he believed to be by Giorgione, for £105.

Many of Lindsay's most important acquisitions were made during the period 1864–75, when he regularly took his family to stay in Florence. William Spence was still eager to offer him assistance in extending his picture collection. Since Lindsay's visit to the city in 1856, Spence had made himself virtually indispensable to Anne Lindsay, whose husband had died in 1855, and he had been rewarded when her daughter, May Holford, elected to make generous use of his services in 1861.[15] Spence was, therefore, well placed to renew business with Lindsay in 1864,[16] and quickly sold him an interesting *Portrait of Giambologna in his Studio* (cat.no.32), which had apparently come from the Guadagni Palace in Florence. This was followed in 1865 by a small picture of the *Crucifixion* now attributed to the Master of the Misericordia (cat.no.6), and a Florentine school fresco attributed to A. Pisano (now in a private collection). Then, in June 1866, Lindsay paid £204 for a half-length male portrait by Van Dyck, and the substantial sum of 900 gold francs for a large altarpiece by the Ferrarese L'Ortolano representing the *Holy Family with St Catherine* (untraced).

Torello Bacci was another Florentine dealer with whom Lindsay established fruitful relations in the 1860s. Lindsay's acquisitions in January 1865 included two fine cassone panels attributed to Jacopo del Sellaio with *Scenes from the Life of Virginia* and *The Death of Lucretia* (cat.no.17); and another pair showing the *Rape of the Sabines* and a scene of *Romans Celebrating* attributed to Dello Delli, which are now at Harewood House, Yorkshire. Towards the end of the same month Bacci also sold Lindsay a tondo representing *Diana and Actaeon*, attributed to Balducci (cat.no.26), and a *Portrait of a Young Woman* attributed to Pollaiuolo. These were followed by a *Tobias and the Angel* attributed to Matteo Rosselli, which was last recorded in the sale of paintings from the Crawford collection at Christie's in October 1946.

Lindsay purchased further pictures in 1865

from a variety of sources. A *Madonna and Child* attributed to Lorenzo di Credi and a *Virgin and Child with Two Angels* by Pinturicchio (cat.no.25) were both apparently bought from the Marchese Frescobaldi in Florence. A fresco fragment of *The Virgin and Child Enthroned* by Domenico Veneziano, now in the National Gallery, London (fig.19), came from the collection of L. Hombert in Florence. A *St Sebastian* attributed to Perugino, now in São Paolo (fig.20), came from a Signor Bruschetti in Milan. A year later, the dealer Tito Gagliardi sold Lindsay an altarpiece of the *Assumption of the Virgin* attributed to Gaudenzio Ferrari for £175. It is now in the Ambrosiana, Milan, where it is catalogued under the name of Giovanni Agostino da Lodi (fig.21).

It was, however, the Lombardi-Baldi collection which provided Lindsay's principal source of pictures both in 1865–6, and again in 1872 and 1875. The residue of the collection was being offered for sale through the Florentine dealer Ludovico Metzger, and in 1865 Lindsay took a *Christ, St John, St Jerome and St Mary of Egypt in a Landscape* by Sellaio, which was then attributed to Andrea del Castagno (cat.no.16); six predella panels representing scenes from the life of Christ, now attributed to Mariotto di Nardo, but then thought to be by Agnolo Gaddi (cat.no.7); and a panel showing the *Death of St Ephraim and other Scenes from the Lives of Hermits* (cat.no.11 or 12), which dates from the second half of the fifteenth century, but which, like the closely related panel acquired from Spence in 1856, was traditionally attributed to Lorenzetti. At this time he bought from the same source a vast glazed terracotta altarpiece then attributed to Lucca della Robbia, and now to his follower Benedetto Buglioni (on loan to the National Museums of Scotland, Edinburgh). In spite of Lindsay's emphasis on sculpture in his *Sketches of the History of Christian Art*, this and a Della Robbia lunette of the *Virgin Adoring the Christ Child* (cat.no.40), also bought from the Lombardi-Baldi collection the following year, were the only examples to which he apparently attached much significance. The other pieces of sculpture in his collection appear to have been acquired in the same casual spirit as the maiolica and other furnishings. Six years later Lindsay returned to Metzger to buy yet another Lombardi-Baldi picture, a Bicci di Lorenzo altarpiece which is now in Westminster Abbey (see fig.25). With it he acquired a panel representing the *Crucifixion* by Ugolino di Nerio (cat.no.3), which had been incorrectly attached to the top of the Bicci di Lorenzo! Two small Bicci di Lorenzo panels representing *The Annunciation* (cat.no.8) were also attached to the top of the altarpiece, although they were probably not part of the original ensemble.

It was also in 1872 that Lindsay bought the Lombardi-Baldi's thirteenth-century triptych, now attributed to Grifo di Tancredi, representing the *Death of St Ephraim* in the centre panel and *Scenes from the Life of Christ* in the wings. The central scene is of considerable iconographic interest as the earliest surviving painting representing hermits and anchorites gathered around the body of St Ephraim, and may be based on a lost Byzantine prototype. This tabernacle was a particularly suitable acquisition for Lindsay's collection, since he already possessed two fifteenth-century panels of the same subject in which the representation of St Ephraim followed the same Byzantine pattern. It may have been at about this time that he acquired from Spence an altarpiece of *The Virgin and Child with Sts John and Verdiana*, which is now attributed to the Master of Santo Spirito (cat.no.20). Lindsay's final addition to the collection, in 1875, was an altarpiece of the *Madonna and Child with Saints* by Signorelli, now in the National Gallery of Art in Washington (fig.22), which, like so many of his best acquisitions, also came from the Lombardi-Baldi collection in Florence.

Important works such as this altarpiece entitle Lindsay to a place among the more enterprising collectors of Italian art in the third quarter of the nineteenth century. Yet it is difficult to escape the feeling that his vision for

the art-historical department of his family museum, which he had outlined in 1849, had not been quite realised, even when allowance is made for the series of copies by Corsi around which the original works of art were to be grouped.

From the outset Lindsay's vision was wholly unrealistic, at least so far as pictures were concerned. It has never been possible to make a satisfactory collection of works of art, each of which is unique, in the same systematic and cerebral manner that may be applied to the task of building up a library of books. If Lindsay had a weakness as a picture collector, it stemmed from his inability to contemplate works of art individually, and in strictly aesthetic terms, rather than as specimens or components in a vast historical or philosophical panorama.

This predilection for abstract thought had, of course, already become apparent in Lindsay's art-historical studies during the 1840s, when he had allowed religious preoccupations to distort the structure of his *Sketches of the History of Christian Art*. Even in his maturity, he was still all too easily intoxicated by a romantic historical notion of intellectual and artistic continuity and progress. Indeed, by the 1860s he had come to regard his own collecting activities, in the fields of both books and pictures, as a direct continuation of the Renaissance tradition of private patronage established by the Medici princes in fifteenth-century Florence. In the library letter of 1861, addressed to his heir Ludovic, he composed a memorable passage on this idea which

Fig.19 · Domenico Veneziano
(active 1438–died 1461)
The Virgin and Child Enthroned
National Gallery, London

Fig.20 · Attributed to Pietro Perugino
(c.1445/50–1523)
St Sebastian
Museu de Arte de São Paolo

eloquently conveys his aristocratic ambitions for his family (see p.15).

If, finally, we turn away from Lindsay's more visionary and dynastic aspirations and concentrate instead on the fundamental character of his picture collection, we find above all a group of exceptionally interesting fourteenth- and fifteenth-century paintings, focused on the early Christian legends and the lives of the saints and martyrs in faraway places, from the Egyptian desert to southern India, which together reflect and illuminate the intellectual character of his book on Christian art – precisely what one might have expected from such an academic art collector. These works, notably the Thebaid triptych (cat.no.1), the fifteenth-century panels with the *Death of St Ephraim* (cat.nos.11 & 12), and the panels by Luca di Tommè, the Master of the Gesuati and attributed to Domenico Ghirlandaio (cat.nos.4, 9 & 15), all enrich Lindsay's profound analyses of the Eastern and Byzantine influences on the mythology and iconography of early Christian art in western Europe. In this important respect his collection was very different in spirit from those of Anglican clergymen such as the Revd Walter Davenport Bromley and the Revd John Fuller Russell, or the Anglo-Catholic landowner Thomas Gambier Parry, who built and then himself decorated a Gothic-revival church at Highnam (1849–51).[17] They were all primarily motivated by sentiment and the 'religious depth of feeling' to be experienced from the works of the early masters – although these qualities were of course also to be found in Lindsay's collection, notably in the Duccio,

Ugolino and Giovanni da Milano Crucifixion scenes (cat.nos.2, 3 and 5). On the other hand, Lindsay's capacity to appreciate classical antiquity both for its own sake and as a source for and influence on medieval art – for instance, in his perceptive comments in 1842 on Piero della Francesca's frescoes at Arezzo – may also have equipped him to express more tolerance than one might have expected for the sensibilities of the next generation of Italophiles, reflected in the aesthetic movement, embodied in the activities of his nephew Coutts, and expressed in literary form in the bitter-sweet writings of Walter Pater on Botticelli and Leonardo da Vinci (1873), where the duality of pagan and Christian thought is made even more explicit. This tendency is arguably anticipated in such Lindsay acquisitions as the Botticelli *St Lawrence* (cat.no.18), the Jacopo del Sellaio panels depicting moral tales from ancient Roman history (cat.no.17) and the Leonardesque *St John the Baptist* (cat.no.30).

1. Open letter concerning the Bibliotheca Lindesiana from Lord Lindsay to his son James Ludovic, dated Florence, February 1865. The 'symbolical pavilion' is clearly an allusion to the ancient family crest of the Lindsay family.

2. Letter to Anne Lindsay, dated Haigh, 10 September 1842.

3. Letter to Miss Jean Trotter, dated Haigh, 24 January 1843. For the 'Fra Angelico' (the attribution of which is no longer universally accepted), see the *Catalogue des Tableaux composant La Gallerie de Feu Son Eminence Le Cardinal Fesch*, Rome, 1841, cat.no.565, and the subsequent sale and public exhibition catalogue by George, Rome, Palazzo Falconieri, 1845, (Part 4), cat.no.660.

4. This copy was sold at Sotheby's, London, 11 April 1990 (lot 213).

5. One of these, after Filippino's *Dispute of Saints Peter and Paul with Simon Magus before Nero*, survives in a British private collection.

6. The latter two copies now belong to the Diocese of Liverpool: the Gentile da Fabriano copy is in Croxteth Parish Church; that after Fra Angelico in Walton Parish Church.

7. For the Revd John Fuller Russell, see H. Liddon, *Life of Edward Bouverie Pusey*, London, 1893-7, I, pp.400–408 and II, pp.141–5. Gustav Waagen (1854, II, p.461) described him as 'one of the most enthusiastic admirers of the grandeur and high significance of the ecclesiastic art from the 13th to the 15th century that I met with in England, being so much impressed with its purity and religious depth of feeling, that the art of the 16th century, with all that fuller development of chiaroscuro, perspective, etc., which too often usurped the place of the true religious aim, is only sparingly admitted into his collection ... So richly are his walls adorned with Italian specimens of the 14th century, that the spectator feels as if transported into a chapel at Siena or Florence'.

8. See F. Haskell 'William Coningham and his collection of Old Masters' in *Burlington Magazine*, CXXXIII, 1991, pp.676–81.

9. E. Joly de Bammeville was a friend of John Henry, later Cardinal Newman. For a brief character sketch of De Bammeville, see A. Pollen, *John Hungerford Pollen*, London, 1912, p.223, who wrote: 'M. de Bammeville proved to be a most agreeable if eccentric companion; and his wife was as pleasant as himself. He soon became intimate with John Pollen, his brother, and his friends and figures in the journal as "Bumvil". He would arrive uninvited, expecting dinner or bed, as often as he failed to come by promise. He was a man of culture and accomplishment, played and sang fine music, and collected beautiful things; his hospitable house in London was filled with superb prints, and pictures well worth seeing; he was a keen judge of character, which he professed to read infallibly in handwriting; and his conversation on men and things was witty and acute ...'. De Bammeville was active as a collector during the 1840s: three fresco scenes by Pinturicchio and Signorelli now in the National Gallery, London, were removed from the walls of the Palazzo del Magnifico in Siena on his instructions in 1842 or 1844.

10. The Revd Walter Davenport was the youngest son of Davies Davenport of Capesthorne and of Charlotte Sneyd. After graduating at Christ Church, Oxford in 1808, he married first Caroline Barbara, daughter of John Gooch of Saxlingham, Archdeacon of Sudbury, and second Lady Louisa Mary Dawson. After inheriting the Bromley family property at Baginton in 1822, he changed his name to Davenport-Bromley. Waagen (1854, III, p.371) described him as 'an ardent admirer of all such pictures, be they of the 13th or 16th century, in which an unaffected and genuine feeling is expressed'.

11. D. Robertson: *Sir Charles Eastlake and the Victorian Art World*, Princeton 1978, pp.136–7, note 55.

12. Unfortunately, many of Spence's accounts and letters to Lord Lindsay are undated. Prices are sometimes quoted in sterling, sometimes in Italian currency. I have not always managed to establish the rate of exchange, and it appears to have fluctuated quite considerably over the years with which we are concerned. For a detailed study of Spence as an art dealer, see J. Fleming in *Burlington Magazine*, CXXI, 1979, pp.500–3, 568–80.

13. Letter to her son, Robert, Florence 4 May 1856.

14. A microfilm is in the Scottish Record Office.

15. May Holford gave a vivid description of her dealings with Spence in a letter to her mother dated Florence, 16 November 1861: 'We have now been here a week to-morrow, and we have been hard at work visiting every shop and picture dealer in the town, always accompanied by Mr. Spence, who arrives every morning soon after breakfast and remains till about 4 o'clock, when it becomes too dark to do anything, and I am thoroughly tired out. We have made some *wonderfully* good acquisitions and I look forward with so much pleasure to showing you them on our return home. Mr. Spence has been of the greatest use to us, as he knows every collection, and every hole and corner of Florence and he is most kind in helping us to find all that we want ... You cannot think how kind and civil everyone is, and from Robert's having built Dorchester House which seems to me to be quite as well known everywhere we go, as it is in England, everyone opens their houses and are so anxious that we should go and see them, and so willing to give us every help possible ... We have been twice to pay Mr. Spence a visit at his Villa at the top of Fiesole, such a charming villa, he has also got a beautiful house in Florence – I quite envy him. Tomorrow we go to see Mario's Villa Salviati and Prince Poniatowski's palace...'.

16. Two letters from Anne Lindsay to May Holford dated Florence, 25 and 27 November 1864, describe further Spence's lodgings (noting two fine Van Dyck portraits), dealing activities ('he gets as much interested in your purchases as if they were his own and becomes quite excited in your behalf') and his social circle (see Brigstocke, 1982, pp.319–20, n.1).

17. Thomas Gambier Parry (1816–88) was a Director of the East India Company and a Gloucestershire landowner. His important collection of early Italian art is now in the Courtauld Institute Gallery, London. He was a member of the Cambridge Camden Society and was deeply concerned with the revival of Gothic art and architecture in Britain. Gambier Parry acknowledges Lindsay's book as a formative influence and visited Assisi on 19 May 1852 'with Lord Lyndsey's [sic] book in hand'. Lindsay, however, would not have approved of the archaic style of the frescos at Highnam. See further D. Farr (ed.), *Thomas Gambier Parry as Artist and Collector*, exhibition catalogue, Courtauld Institute Galleries, London, 1993, pp.30ff., n.18.

1

GRIFO DI TANCREDI

active 1271–1303

A Triptych

Central panel: The Death of St Ephraim with Scenes from the Lives of the Thebaid Saints. In the gable above: Christ the Redeemer Blessing with Six Angels. In the wings: Six Scenes from the Passion of Christ: (left) Mourning Angels, the Crucifixion and the Three Maries at the Tomb; (right) the Flagellation; the Mocking of Christ and the Descent into Limbo.

Panel, overall dimensions with wings open: 118.5 × 124.5 cm. Central panel: 112 × 62 cm (including mouldings); left wing: 87.4 × 30.9 cm; right wing: 87.8 × 31 cm

Some of the wooden mouldings of the central panel have been replaced, and those enclosing the fragmentary base-block are also modern (probably nineteenth century). The hinges attaching the wings are modern but X-rays demonstrate that the wings were always part of the original structure.

Inscribed on the base-block: ... h[oc] op[us] q[uod?] fec[it] m[agister] Gri[fus] Fl[orentinus]

There is no imagery on the reverse of the panels: the central panel has a green wash over a gesso ground; the wings are painted dark blue with gold stars.

PROVENANCE: Lombardi-Baldi collection, Florence; (no.4 in the 1845 catalogue); bought by Lord Lindsay from their executor, Ludovico Metzger, on 4 June 1872, as anonymous Florentine.

PRIVATE COLLECTION
On loan to the National Gallery of Scotland since 1979

1. See G. Achenbach, 'An Early Italian Tabernacle', in Gazette des Beaux-Arts, XXV, 1944, pp.129–32.

2. J. R. Martin, 'The Death of St Ephraim in Byzantine and Early Italian Painting' in Art Bulletin, XXXIII, 1951, pp.217–25.

The form of this tabernacle triptych, with its cusped romanesque arch moulding, appears to be unique in Italian painting of this period.

The central panel is focused on the death of St Ephraim of Syria (died 373), with St Gregory of Nicea reading the funeral sermon, and with other saints and desert hermits either travelling to his funeral, shown at the bottom, or witnessing the vision of four angels carrying his soul to heaven, shown at the very top. To the left, at the lowest level of the composition, there is a group of mourning monks, one of whom rings the bells and another strikes the simandra. The subsidiary scenes represent incidents in the lives of other early hermits living in the Egyptian desert, known as the Thebaid. These include, on the left, St Jerome and the lion; St Anthony Abbot (died 356) looking out of his hut at a woman presented by the devil; toward the centre, St John the Recluse administered to by angels. In the centre above the funeral scene there is a stylite on his column, probably Simeon the Stylite (died 459). Other scenes are probably generic, simply illustrating aspects of life in the desert, and the birds and animals who inhabited it. For instance, we find shepherds chasing away a wolf in the area immediately above the funeral, while at the upper right a hermit is milking a goat. The literary sources for these incidents, which date from the fifth century, are the *Vitas Patrum*, traditionally attributed to St Jerome, and the *Paradise Fathers* or *Lausiac History* by Palladius, Bishop of Helenopolis. Later in the Middle Ages these stories were incorporated into such compilations as *The Golden Legend* by Jacopo da Voragine (c.1230–1298), Archbishop of Genoa, and Domenico Cavalca's *Volgarizzamento delle vite de Santi Padri*.[1]

The central panel with the *Death of St Ephraim* is probably based on a lost Byzantine prototype, although the earliest surviving Byzantine examples date from as late as the sixteenth century.[2] Isolated scenes from the *Death of St Ephraim* composition can, however, be traced individually to eleventh-century Byzantine manuscripts of *The Heavenly Ladder* by John Climacus, and in particular to one in the Vatican (Ms. Gr 394) and to the Princeton Climax manuscript. These scenes were probably fused by a later Byzantine artist into a single and presumably famous composition, centred around the death of St Ephraim, on which subsequent Byzantine versions were then invariably based. The present picture, of Tuscan origin and dating from the late thirteenth century, is the earliest surviving

Fig.23 · X-ray detail showing the pentimento in the upper right of the central panel where the large tree has been painted over a building.

painting showing the *Death of St Ephraim* within the Byzantine tradition. The gable and wings, on the other hand, are derived iconographically from Italian thirteenth-century prototypes, including Cimabue's *Crucifixion* fresco in the left transept of the upper church of San Francesco at Assisi.

This triptych has been identified as the work of an anonymous artist known as the 'Maestro di San Gaggio' from his *Madonna and Four Saints* in the Accademia, Florence, which originates from the Florentine church of San Gaggio.[3] Other works by this hand include a triptych in the Gemäldegalerie, Berlin, and the wings of a dossal (a panel painting hung in front of or behind an altar) at San Diego, California. More recently it has been proposed, on the basis of the inscription on the present picture, that the 'Maestro di San Gaggio' might be Grifo di Tancredi, an artist recorded in a document of 1295.[4] Although the inscription on Lord Lindsay's picture is incomplete and difficult to read, this identification has found wide acceptance. In any event, the artist appears to have been close to both Cimabue and Giotto and may have trained under the Magdalen Master, who painted the central panel of the San Diego dossal mentioned above. He had the capacity to breathe new life into Roman and Byzantine forms and in the present picture achieves a manner of considerable emotional and expressive power.

It has been suggested that more than one hand may have been involved in the execution of this triptych, partly on the grounds that the wings and the figures of Christ and the angels in the gable are painted on a larger scale and with a less meticulous technique than the figures in the Thebaid at the centre.[5] Although one cannot exclude a studio collaboration similar to that noted in the San Diego dossal, close comparative examination of the treatment of such details as the angels' wings at the top of the Thebaid, in the gable, and in the Crucifixion scene, would suggest that all these sections are the work of one artist. The principal differences are due to the obvious variations of scale and the fact that the central panel is derived from a separate iconographical tradition.

One interesting technical feature of the central panel is a significant pentimento at the upper right, where the large tree has been painted over a building, which can be detected through the foliage with the naked eye, and much more clearly in an X-ray of the painting (fig.23). This indicates that the artist was not simply slavishly following an existing design.

3. For the 'Maestro di San Gaggio', see R. Longhi, 'Giudizio sul Duecento' in *Proporzioni*, II, 1948, pp.1–34. For the attribution of the Lindsay panel to this hand, see Bellosi, 1974, p.20, n.15; A. Tartuferi, *La Pittura in Italia: Il Duecento e il Trecento*, I, *Pittura fiorentina del Duecento*, 1986, pp.267–82; A. Tartuferi, *La Pittura a Firenze nel Duecento*, 1990, pp.107–8.

4. For the attribution to Grifo di Tancredi, see M. Boskovits, *Katalog der Gemälde: Frühe Italienische Malerei*, Berlin, 1988, pp.122–4, under cat.no.48; R. Bagemihl, 'Some Thoughts about Grifo di Tancredi of Florence and a little-known panel at Volterra', in *Arte Cristiana*, LXXXVII, 1999, pp.413–26. For the document of 1295, see R. Davidsohn, *Forschungen zur Geschichte von Florenz*, Berlin, 1901, III, p.225.

5. In a letter to the owner from Colin Thompson, former Director of the National Galleries of Scotland, dated 13 April 1981.

2

ATTRIBUTED TO
DUCCIO DI BUONINSEGNA
active 1278 – died before August 1319

The Crucifixion

Panel, 59.7 × 38 cm

PROVENANCE: E. Joly de Bammeville; his sale,
Christie's, London, 12 June 1854 (lot 54), as by Duccio;
bought by the Revd Walter Davenport for 265 guineas;
his sale, Christie's, London, 12 June 1863 (lot 52), as by
Duccio; bought by 'Anthony' for Lord Lindsay for 250
guineas; by descent in the family until sold at
Christie's, London, 2 July 1976 (lot 95), as by Duccio;
acquired by Manchester City Art Gallery with the aid of
the National Art Collections Fund, 1984.

EXHIBITIONS: London, 1893, cat.no.21, as by Duccio;
London, 1904, cat.no.4, as by Duccio; London, 1930,
cat.no.5, as by Duccio.

LENT BY MANCHESTER CITY ART GALLERIES

The scene is depicted as described in the gospels,
with Christ on the cross between the two
thieves, the swooning Virgin supported by the
two Maries at the lower left, a grieving St John
in red at the foot of the cross and behind him,
also in red, the Magdalen with arms upraised.
At the lower right, the artist includes both the
Roman centurion who, according to the gospels
of Matthew, Mark and Luke, exclaimed that
Jesus truly was the Son of God; and also, behind,
the soldier who pierced Christ's side with a
spear, as described in St John's gospel. Although
there was a tendency among artists to conflate
these two figures, here the distinction is clearly
made. The standing soldier who clasps the
spear, still red with Christ's blood, also holds his
bloody right hand to his eyes. His failing eye-
sight was thus miraculously restored, as described by Jacopo da Voragine in *The Golden
Legend*.

Although the traditional attribution of this
panel to Duccio long went unchallenged,[1] more
recent scholarly opinion has been polarised over
the issue of its authorship, with a majority
coming down in favour of an attribution to one
of his pupils or followers. The names of Segna di
Bonaventura (active 1298(?) – died before 1331)[2]
and Ugolino di Nerio (see following entry),[3] for
example, have been put forward. This conclusion hinges on a detailed analysis of the artistic
sources on which the author of the Lindsay
panel drew, and of the manner in which these
differ from those drawn upon by Duccio for the
Crucifixion scene in the documented *Maestà*
(fig.24).[4] Details of both works betray a knowledge of certain seminal prototypes, such as the
frescoed *Crucifixion* by Cimabue in the south
transept of the Upper Church of San Francesco
at Assisi, and the sculpted ones by Nicola Pisano
on the pulpit in Siena Cathedral and by
Giovanni Pisano at Pistoia. The fact that the two
compositions adapt different elements from
these (and other) sources, is taken as evidence
that they are by different hands. And although
the author of the Lindsay panel is recognised as
an artist of considerable stature, with a capacity
for iconographic and formal innovation (for
example, in the partly obscured back view of
Longinus), some of the figure types and certain
technical details – such as the character of the
underdrawing, and the tooling of the haloes –
are judged to be untypical of Duccio's workshop. This argument concludes, somewhat
frustratingly, by assigning the Manchester
panel to a distinctive but anonymous follower

of Duccio working around 1330, to whom no
other surviving works can be attributed.

The alternative view is that the present panel
is, as nineteenth-century connoisseurs believed, a
late work by Duccio himself, executed during the
years between the completion of the *Maestà* in
the summer of 1311, and the artist's death seven
or eight years later.[5] No paintings by Duccio can
be securely dated to this period, and there is,
therefore, scope for speculation about possible
technical and stylistic developments in his late
style. According to this argument, an artist of his
stature and capacity for creative innovation
would not necessarily have restricted himself to a
single iconographic pattern in his successive
interpretations of the Crucifixion subject.

The issue of the attribution of this beautiful,
moving and excellently preserved panel will not
easily be resolved but the detailed stylistic
arguments are of more than academic interest,
for they serve to focus attention on the painting's
expressive qualities which would have inspired
Lord Lindsay.

Fig.24 · Duccio di Buoninsegna (active 1278–died before
August 1319)
The Crucifixion from the *Maestà* altarpiece
Museo dell'Opera del Duomo, Siena

1. Among those who have endorsed the attribution to
Duccio are Crowe and Cavalcaselle, 1864, II, p.52, n.1;
idem, 1908 (edited by R. Langton Douglas), III, pp.18–19;
and Berenson, 1968, I, p.116.

2. For the attribution to Segna, see A. Venturi, *Storia dell'
Arte Italiana*, v, 1907, pp.574, 578 n.1; Van Marle, II, 1924,
pp.139–40, n.9.

3. For the attribution to Ugolino see J. Stubblebine, *Duccio
and his School*, Princeton, 1979, pp.174–5 (as a late work,
dating from no earlier than c.1330).

4. For a full discussion, see J. White, *Duccio*, 1979, pp.151–7
(as circle of Duccio).

5. See P. Pouncey, 'A Sienese 14th-century Crucifixion', in
National Art-Collections Fund Review, 1985, pp.133–5.

3

UGOLINO DI NERIO
(UGOLINO DA SIENA)
active 1317 – died 1339/1349

The Crucifixion with the Virgin and St John the Evangelist

Panel, 105 × 47.5 cm

The panel appears to have been cut up and then reassembled, and is clearly cut down along the bottom edge. The figures of the Virgin and St John are painted on sections measuring approximately 52 × 18 cm each, which have been inserted back into the central panel with the Crucified Christ. A similar insertion, 12 cm wide at its base, affects the apex of the panel above the cross.

An old label on the reverse is inscribed:
Domenico Ghirlandaio

PROVENANCE: Lombardi-Baldi collection, Florence; bought by Lord Lindsay through their executor Ludovico Metzger in 1872.

PRIVATE COLLECTION

1. The Bicci di Lorenzo altarpiece is described in the Lombardi-Baldi catalogue (under Lorenzo di Bicci) with the two Bicci di Lorenzo pinnacles of the *Annunciation* (cat.no.8) and with a *Crucifixion* in the centre, the description of which does not match the Ugolino panel exhibited here. This could be a case of careless cataloguing, or else the present picture might for some reason have been substituted later. This would explain how a work by Ugolino found its way onto a Bicci di Lorenzo altarpiece. The entry reads: 'Les trois pyramides répresentent: celui du milieu le Christ sur la Croix, avec les trois Maries, les deux autres aux côtés l'Annonciation.' See *Collection de Tableaux Anciens de M. François Lombardi et Hugues Baldi* [1845].

2. See H. Maginnis, 'The Thyssen-Bornemisza Ugolino', in *Apollo*, CXVIII, 1983, pp.16–21.

3. See Boskovits, 1990, cat.no.29. See also G. Coor Achenbach, 'Contributions to the study of Ugolino di Nerio's Art', in *Art Bulletin*, XXXVII, 1955, pp.163–4.

4. For the reconstruction of this altarpiece, see Davies and Gordon, 1988, pp.99–116.

5. Reproduced by Davies and Gordon, 1988, fig.22.

6. Boskovits, 1990, cat.no.29

7. J. Stubblebine, *Duccio and his School*, Princeton, 1979, p.162, fig.391 (as by Ugolino and dated to the mid-1320s).

At the time of its acquisition by Lord Lindsay, this panel formed the pinnacle to a Bicci di Lorenzo altarpiece originating from the Compagni chapel in Santa Trinita, Florence, and now in Westminster Abbey, London (fig.25). This improbable marriage may have taken place while both works were in the Lombardi-Baldi collection (see also cat.no.8).[1] We cannot be sure that the present picture was originally conceived as a pinnacle for any altarpiece, but to judge from its shape this seems likely. Alternatively, it might have formed an integral part of a polyptych; or have been conceived as a portable work for private devotion; or even, as has been suggested recently, have been the principal panel of a small public altarpiece, although it would have been innovatory to use a Crucifixion scene as the main feature at such an early date.[2]

Both in style and conception the Lindsay *Crucifixion* relates extremely closely to a slightly larger *Crucifixion with the Virgin and St John the Evangelist and Six Flying Angels*, now in the Museo Thyssen-Bornemisza, Madrid (fig.26).[3] The principal figures are almost identical, and both pictures have the same distinctive treatment of the cross, painted in blue, as a flat silhouette against the gold ground. The Madrid picture is now widely recognised as a key work for our understanding of Ugolino, a pupil and follower of Duccio whose principal surviving documented work, a polyptych from Santa Croce, Florence, dating from *c*.1325–30, is now dispersed.[4] The Lindsay picture is certainly by the same hand.

Both *Crucifixions* differ from the surviving panels from the Santa Croce polyptych in the treatment of the haloes. Whereas the ex-Santa Croce panels have punched decoration, the *Crucifixion* panels have haloes that were carefully incised with a stylus in a more traditional manner. This might indicate they are earlier in date. It also appears to rule out speculation that the Lindsay *Crucifixion* might be the lost pinnacle of the Santa Croce polyptych, which according to a reproductive drawing made for the French historian Séroux d'Agincourt also represented the *Crucifixion*.[5] The starker flesh tones in the Lindsay panel, which lack the distinctive green and pink highlights of the figures in the surviving ex-Santa Croce panels, also suggest that this *Crucifixion* was conceived for a separate purpose. It has been proposed that, on account of 'the slower linear rhythms of its design and its more static quality', the Lindsay panel may be slightly earlier than the Madrid *Crucifixion*, where 'the artist seems ... to aspire towards a more ample

plastic treatment of form', and 'accentuates the chiaroscuro contrasts and rhythmic emphasis not only in the agitated flying angels but also in the draperies enveloping the figures in large deep folds'.[6]

Of the two, it is the Lindsay panel, without the chorus of angels, that presents the starker, more contemplative image and which emancipates itself further from the more dramatic and crowded Crucifixion scenes on the reverse side of Duccio's *Maestà* and in the panel from Manchester (see previous entry). The chronological sequence of Ugolino's paintings is far from clear, but all the pictures discussed here were apparently painted in the third decade of the fourteenth century.[7]

Fig.25 · Bicci di Lorenzo (1373–1452)
The Virgin and Child Enthroned with Saints
Westminster Abbey, London

The photograph shows the polyptych as it was when Lord Lindsay bought it, with Ugolino di Nerio's *Crucifixion* and Bicci di Lorenzo's *Annunciation* forming the pinnacles.

Fig.26 · Ugolino di Nerio (active 1317–died 1339/49)
The Crucifixion with the Virgin and St John the Evangelist and Six Flying Angels
Museo Thyssen-Bornemisza, Madrid

4

LUCA DI TOMMÈ
active 1356–1389

Four Scenes from the Life of St Thomas

[A] *Christ and St Thomas at Cesarea meet Abanes, the messenger from King Gondoforus of the Indies, who needs workmen to build a palace*

Panel, 32 × 32.2 cm

[B] *A butler strikes St Thomas at a wedding feast; the butler's severed hand is then brought to St Thomas in the mouth of a dog*

Panel, 32.6 × 33.5 cm

[C] *St Thomas in prison; St Thomas baptises Gondoforus after the king's brother Gad had risen from the dead*

Panel, 32.2 × 34 cm

[D] *The Broken Idol; St Thomas stabbed by the High Priest*

Panel, 32.5 × 34.5 cm

PROVENANCE: Thomas Blayds; his sale, Christie's, London 31 March 1849 (lots 192, 193, 198, 199), as by Giotto; bought by 'Harris' for Lord Lindsay.

EXHIBITION: London, *Italian Art and Britain*, 1960, cat.no.270.

PRIVATE COLLECTION
On loan to the National Gallery of Scotland since 1988

St Thomas, one of Christ's Apostles, was a Galilean fisherman who refused to believe in the resurrection until he had seen and touched the wounds of the risen Christ, a subject often depicted in Western art. The predella panels from Lord Lindsay's collection illustrate the less familiar story of St Thomas's sea journey to southern India, his foundation of a Christian church there, and his eventual martyrdom. Although this story, taken from *The Golden Legend* of Jacopo da Voragine and based on the apocryphal 'Acts of Saint Thomas', is often dismissed as legendary, it might well be based on an actual journey to Kerala. The Christians of Malabar have always claimed that they were evangelised by St Thomas and that he was buried at Mylapore near Madras. Lord Lindsay probably bought these panels because of their iconographical interest. In his *Sketches* (I, p.cxcvii), he cites the second book of Odericus Vitalis as his primary source of information about the life of St Thomas. Mrs Jameson also gives a comprehensive and more colourful account of the story in her *Sacred and Legendary Art* (I, pp.224–7).

After arriving in India, St Thomas was imprisoned for distributing to the poor money intended for King Gondoforus's palace. However, he had built him a heavenly palace instead, which was revealed to the king's brother Gad, who rose from the dead to describe it. Thomas was released and the king was baptised, but eventually St Thomas was martyred after refusing to worship pagan idols which fell to the ground at his bidding.

These four scenes are panels from the predella of an altarpiece. A fifth panel, which would have been at the centre of the predella, has been identified as a *Crucifixion* in the Pinacoteca Vaticana in Rome (fig.27).[1] It is of oblong format, but has exactly the same pattern of framing as the panels from Lord Lindsay's collection. There has been wide agreement that these panels are by the Sienese painter Luca di Tommè, who inherited the stylistic conventions of Simone Martini and Pietro and Ambrogio Lorenzetti, and helped sustain the Sienese tradition of clear composition and graceful line. It seems likely that this predella was originally attached to a polyptych now in the Pinacoteca Nazionale, Siena, which shows *The Virgin and Child Enthroned with Sts John the Baptist, Thomas, Benedict and Stephen* (fig.28). The altarpiece entered the Siena gallery in 1842 and the predella was probably detached and sold off shortly before. In view of its iconography, the polyptych might originally have been in the convent church of San Tommaso degli Umiliati

in Siena. It is signed and dated on the decorative framing: NICCHOLAUS SER SOCCII ET LUCAS TOMAS DE SENIS HOC OPUS PINSUERUNT ANNI MCCCLXII (Niccolò di Ser Sozzo and Luca di Tommè of Siena painted this work in the year 1362).[2] While critics are divided about the respective roles of the two painters in designing and executing the principal panels of the polyptych, this does not extend to the predella by Luca di Tommè.[3]

Fig.27 · Luca di Tommè (active 1356–1389)
The Crucifixion
Pinacoteca Vaticana, Rome

Fig.28 · Luca di Tommè (active 1356–1389)
The Virgin and Child Enthroned with Sts John the Baptist, Thomas, Benedict and Stephen
Pinacoteca Nazionale, Siena

1. F. Zeri, 'Sul Problema di Niccolò Tegliacci e Luca di Tomè' in *Paragone*, 105, 1958, pp.3–6.

2. Fehm, 1986, pp.13, 80, cat.no.13.

3. M. Meiss, 'Notes on Three Linked Sienese Styles' in *Art Bulletin*, XLV, 1963, p.48; Fehm, 1986, p.76, cat.no.11; Berenson, 1968, I, p.224.

5

GIOVANNI DA MILANO
active 1346–1369

The Crucifixion with the Three Maries, St John the Evangelist and other Saints, and Flying Angels

Panel, 50.7 × 35.5 cm (original panel); 63 × 45 cm (including the nineteenth-century engaged frame). The panel is gessoed on the reverse, with a green border.

PROVENANCE: Bought in Rome by Lord Lindsay in 1842.

PRIVATE COLLECTION

This little known *Crucifixion*, here exhibited in public for the first time, is clearly by the same hand as a *Crucifixion with the Virgin, the Holy Women and Sts John the Evangelist and Francis of Assisi* until recently in the collection of the New York Historical Society (fig.29).[1] The design also relates to a drawing attributed to Giovanni da Milano in the Kupferstichkabinett, Berlin (fig.30).[2] The New York picture was formerly owned by the well known nineteenth-century French collector Artaud de Montor who, in his catalogue of 1811, attributed it to Botticelli.[3] The attribution to Giovanni da Milano dates from 1905.[4] The picture from Lord Lindsay's collection is much less well known and was only recently recognised as by the same hand as the New York picture.[5] Both may be relatively early works.

Giovanni di Jacopo di Guido da Caversaccio, known as Giovanni da Milano, came from Lombardy but is first recorded on 17 October 1346 among the foreign painters living in Florence. His earliest signed work, a polyptych in the Pinacoteca at Prato, was commissioned by 1363. This was followed by a *Pietà* dated 1365, now in the Accademia, Florence. He was influenced by the Sienese painter Simone Martini, but his forms have a solidity and simplicity that looks back to Giotto. This is particularly true of the Lindsay *Crucifixion*, which lacks the linear grace associated with Giovanni da Milano's mature style, as seen for instance in the *Christ of the Apocalypse, the Virgin and St John the Baptist* in the National Gallery, London.

Fig.29 · Giovanni da Milano (active 1346–1369)
The Crucifixion with the Virgin, the Holy Women and Sts John the Evangelist and Francis of Assisi
Location unknown

Fig.30 · Giovanni da Milano (active 1346–1369)
The Crucifixion with the Three Maries
Kupferstichkabinett, Berlin

1. Sold Sotheby's, New York, 12 January 1995 (lot 14), as by Giovanni da Milano.

2. Inv.no.KdZ4290. See H.T. Schulze Altcappenberg, *Die italienischen Zeichnungen des 14. und 15. Jahrhunderts im Berliner Kupferstichkabinett*, Berlin, 1995, pp.32–4.

3. A.F. Artaud de Montor, *Considerations sur l'état de la peinture en Italie*, 1811, pp.64–5, as Botticelli; idem, *Peintres primitifs: Collection de tableaux rapportée d'Italie*, 1843, p.48, cat.no.138, pl.54.

4. W. Suida, *Florentinische Maler und die Mitte des 14. Jahrhunderts*, 1905, pp.34, 50, as Giovanni da Milano. See further R. Offner, 'Italian Pictures at the New York Historical Society II' in *Art in America*, VII, 1919, pp.190–93; Boskovits, 1971, p.58, n. 4, as an early work; J. Polzer, 'The Master of the Rebel Angels Reconsidered' in *Art Bulletin*, 63, 1981, p.566, as Giovanni da Milano.

5. See Boskovits, 1971, p.58, n.4; C. Travi, in M. Gregori (ed.), *Pittura a Como e nel Canton Ticino dal Mille al Settecento*, Milan, 1994, p.262, as Giovanni da Milano. On the other hand M. Gregori, 'Giovanni da Milano: Storia di un Polittico', in *Paragone*, 265, 1972, p.32, n.61, classifies both the Lord Lindsay and the ex-New York *Crucifixions* as by a Lombard follower of Giovanni da Milano.

6

THE MASTER OF THE MISERICORDIA
active in the last quarter of the
fourteenth century

The Crucifixion with the Virgin Mary and Saints

In the base below: The Madonna and Child between Sts Venieri and Crescentino

The predella at the bottom, with weakly executed scenes from the life of Christ (*Agony in the Garden, Flagellation, Christ Carrying the Cross, Deposition, Noli me Tangere*), does not belong to the original ensemble, and probably dates from no earlier than 1500. The gilt framing elements of which this predella forms part is a reconstruction, probably dating from the nineteenth century.

Original painted panel, with arched top, including the upper base, 87.8 × 50 cm

Inscribed on an old label on the reverse: *Pupil of Giottino.*

PROVENANCE: William Spence, Florence; from whom bought by Lord Lindsay on 3 January 1865.

PRIVATE COLLECTION

The *Crucifixion* is here not represented as a strictly historical event, for several of the attendant saints were certainly not present, and are presumably included in a symbolic or intercessory role. The artist establishes a clear distinction between the grief-stricken foreground figures of the Virgin, Mary Magdalen (who embraces the blood-streaked shaft of the cross) and St John the Evangelist, all of whom witnessed the events of Christ's Passion, and the four later saints behind, whose expressions and gestures are more neutral. Of the latter, the two bishop saints with mitres and croziers, and the crusader saint at the right with a long sword, cannot be identified with any certainty. Only St Catherine of Alexandria, at the left, is clearly identified by her traditional attributes, a book, a martyr's palm and, most distinctively, the spiked wheel on which she was tortured. St Catherine (died 307) was an early Christian martyr who refused demands by the Emperor Maxentius to make sacrifices to pagan gods, was tortured on a wheel (which miraculously broke into pieces) and was finally beheaded. Her legend is described in some detail by Lord Lindsay in the *Sketches* (I, pp.lxxxiii-viii).

This panel was acquired by Lord Lindsay as the work of Giottino and was later attributed to the circle of Orcagna (Andrea di Cione). It may be compared, for instance, with the *Crucifixion* of c.1366–8 by Jacopo di Cione (youngest brother of Andrea) and his workshop in the National Gallery in London, where one finds an even more elaborate and crowded arrangement of figures, placed in the foreground around the cross, and a similar weakness in the projection of three-dimensional space. The Lindsay picture has now been identified as the work of the anonymous but distinctive artist who painted the *Madonna della Misericordia* in the Galleria dell'Accademia, Florence.[1] He was a Florentine painter whose style was based mainly on that of the Cione workshop, but was also influenced by Taddeo Gaddi, Bernardo Daddi, Giottino and Giovanni da Milano.

1. Boskovits, 1975, p.367. For earlier attributions, see Van Marle, III, p.508, as by Jacopo di Cione; R. Offner, *A Critical Corpus of Florentine Painting*, section III, vol.v, 1947, p.249, as by a follower of Orcagna; Berenson, 1963, I, p.213, as close to Lorenzo di Niccolo.

7

MARIOTTO DI NARDO

1394–1424

Six Scenes from the Life of Christ

[A] *The Annunciation*

Panel (octagonal), 30.2 × 30.5 cm

[B] *The Adoration of the Shepherds*

Panel (octagonal), 28.2 × 33.2 cm, including additions to the upper right and extreme right edges, which are made up to a maximum of 1 cm

[C] *The Adoration of the Magi*

Panel (octagonal), 28.8 × 33.5 cm

[D] *The Presentation in the Temple*

Panel (octagonal), 30.4 × 30.5 cm

[E] *Christ among the Doctors*

Panel (octagonal), 30.5 × 30.6 cm

[F] *The Baptism of Christ*

Panel (octagonal), 31 × 31 cm, including additions to the bottom three sides, which are made up to a maximum of 1.7 cm

Old labels on the reverse of each panel are inscribed: *History of Our Saviour by Angelo Gaddi, about 1370.*

PROVENANCE: Lombardi-Baldi collection, Florence (nos.15–20 in the 1845 catalogue, as by Agnolo Gaddi); bought by Lord Lindsay from their executor, Ludovico Metzger, on 17 January 1865 for 180 francs, as by Agnolo Gaddi.

PRIVATE COLLECTION

These six panels with scenes from the early life of Christ presumably originally formed the predella of an altarpiece, which has not been identified. The attribution to Mariotto di Nardo is widely accepted.[1] The presence of two Franciscan friars masquerading as shepherds in the Nativity scene is an unusual feature, and may offer a clue to the original provenance of the pictures. Another predella panel by Mariotto representing the *Adoration of the Magi* in the Allen Memorial Art Museum, Oberlin, is closely related to the equivalent Lindsay panel both in style and in the design of the Virgin and Child and the two kings nearest to them. Mariotto di Nardo, the son of a sculptor, worked in a conservative and traditional style with a capacity for clear story-telling, without ornament or fantasy. He worked in Florence at the Cathedral, in Santa Maria Maggiore and at Orsanmichele.

1. R. Offner, 'The 'Mostra del Tesoro di Firenze Sacra': II' in *Burlington Magazine*, LXIII, 1933, p.169, n.4; M. Eisenberg 'A Partial Reconstruction of a Predella by Mariotto di Nardo' in *Allen Memorial Art Museum Bulletin*, IX, 1, 1951 pp.9–10; Berenson, 1963, I, p.129; Boskovits, 1975, p.389.

A

D

B

C

E

F

8

BICCI DI LORENZO
1373–1452

The Angel of the Annunciation

Panel, 63.5 × 32.2 cm

The Virgin Annunciate

Panel, 64 × 32.6 cm

Inscribed on a nineteenth-century label on the reverse:
Lorenzo di Bicci.

The present frames probably date from the nineteenth
century.

PRIVATE COLLECTION

The iconography of the Annunciation, with the
Virgin seated, dates from early Christian times
and was traditional in fourteenth- and fifteenth-
century Tuscany. The influence of the popular
Meditations on the Life of Christ by the Franciscan
writer known as the Pseudo Bonaventura is
reflected in the idea of Gabriel flying toward the
Virgin, and in the bible opened at the words of
the prophet Isaiah (7:14): 'Ecce Virgo concipiet'.

At the time of acquisition by Lord Lindsay,
these panels formed the pinnacles of a Bicci di
Lorenzo altarpiece of the *Madonna and Child with
Sts Anthony Abbott, Giovanni Gualberto, John the
Baptist and Catherine*, painted in 1433–4 for the
Compagni chapel in Santa Trinita, Florence,
which was also acquired by Lindsay (it is now in
Westminster Abbey, fig.25).[1] They were subsequently removed, together with the *Crucifixion* by
Ugolino (cat.no.3), which had been placed in the
centre between these two panels of the *Annunciation* (see fig.25). Although it is tempting to speculate that the *Annunciation* panels may originally
have formed part of the Santa Trinita altarpiece,
comparison of the punching of the haloes, which
is of a different pattern, militates against this
conclusion.

The two panels of the *Annunciation* are very
similar in design to two other panels of the same
subject by Bicci di Lorenzo now in the Museo
Thyssen-Bornemisza, Madrid (fig.31 a–c).[2] These
were almost certainly originally two pinnacles of
a polyptych, and flanked a central pinnacle
representing the *Crucifixion*, also in the Museo
Thyssen-Bornemisza. A polyptych by Mariotto di
Nardo dating from 1393–4, of precisely this

format and with identical subject-matter, is in
the Galleria dell'Accademia, Florence, and offers
the most likely model for the original setting of
the Lindsay *Annunciation* panels. The principal
differences between the Madrid and Lindsay
panels are iconographic. In the former, the dove
of the Holy Spirit is shown above the Virgin, and
God the Father is shown pointing above the
figure of the angel. They have been dated on
stylistic evidence to around 1430, shortly after a
triptych of 1427 in the Archivio Capitolare in
Florence Cathedral, and therefore a little earlier
than the altarpiece now in Westminster Abbey.
There is no dispute surrounding the attribution
to Bicci di Lorenzo of either the present pictures
or the similar panels at Madrid. Bicci di Lorenzo's
workshop, founded by his father Lorenzo di Bicci,
was highly productive but conservative in style,
free from Renaissance innovations.

Fig.31 a–c · Bicci di Lorenzo (1373–1452)
*The Angel of the Annunciation; The Crucifixion; The Virgin
Annunciate*
Museo Thyssen-Bornemisza, Madrid

1. C. Frosini, 'Il trittico Compagni' in *Scritti in onore di
    Roberto Salvini*, Florence, 1984, pp.227–31.

2. Boskovits, 1990, cat.no.6. By coincidence the Madrid
    picture was also in Scotland in Lindsay's day, having
    been bought by the Scottish artist and speculator James
    Irvine for Sir William Forbes of Pitsligo in 1827, as by
    Giottino. For Irvine's acquisition of this picture
    (hitherto unidentified) from the Florentine dealer
    Nocchi see H. Brigstocke, *William Buchanan and the
    Nineteenth-Century Art Trade: 100 letters to his Agents in London
    and Italy*, London, 1982, pp.26–8. In a letter in a private
    collection dated 9 February 1828, Irvine wrote to Sir
    William: 'When I was in Florence last I bought of
    Nocchi for 50 francisconi a very fine work by Giottino,
    scholar of Giotto, which supposing *too ancient* to send to
    you I proposed taking to Rome; but as you have
    expressed yourself so much in favour of the older
    masters I have had it put in the case with the
    Rembrandt ... There is an old gothic frame with three
    points and the pointing is in the most perfect
    preservation with figures of grace and expression
    united with simplicity.' There is no evidence as to
    whether Lord Lindsay ever saw the painting.

9

MASTER OF THE GESUATI
active in Ferrara, mid-fifteenth century

St Jerome Removing a Thorn from the Paw of a Lion

Panel, 29.7 × 36.4 cm
PROVENANCE: Unknown

PRIVATE COLLECTION

The story of St Jerome as told by Lord Lindsay is based largely on the account in De Natalibus, although it is also to be found in Jacopo da Voragine's *The Golden Legend* (*Sketches*, I, pp.clxvii-clxxi):

'Jerome, Presbyter and Doctor, was born in Dalmatia, and received full instruction in Greek, Latin and Hebrew letters. But loving Plato more than the prophets, as more polished and elegant in style, and being seized with a fever, so that, the heat of life failing, his death was expected, he was suddenly caught up in the spirit before the judgement seat of God, and being questioned as to his condition, and answering, "a Christian", it was replied, "Thou liest! thou art a Ciceronian, for where thy treasure is, there thy heart is also". And Jerome was silent, and the judge commanded him to be scourged severely.'

Jerome later took himself to the Egyptian desert and then built a monastery at Bethlehem, where he spent fifty years translating the scriptures.

'And on a certain day, towards evening, while Jerome with the brethren were seated reading the Scriptures, a lion which had fallen lame entered the monastery. All fled, and the holy Doctor received him alone, and found that his paw had been wounded by thorns. And after drawing them forth, the lion recovered and thereafter dwelt there like a domestic animal, and ate hay like an ox; on whom Jerome imposed the service of conducting and protecting on the road and in the forest, the ass which brought fire-wood for the monastery'.

Unfortunately the ass was stolen by passing merchants while the lion was asleep and as punishment the lion, who was presumed to have eaten the ass, was thereafter made to carry out the duties of the ass. Later the lion found the ass and drove it and the merchants' camels to the monastery. The merchants came to the abbot to seek pardon and were duly entertained by Jerome, who advised them to respect the property of others.

The present picture appears to relate closely to four other panels depicting further episodes from St Jerome's life.[1] Two paintings in the Pinacoteca di Brera, Milan, show, respectively, the sick saint being chastised before Christ, and the merchants who had stolen the ass apologising to Jerome; another, in a private collection in Turin, shows him praying in the desert; and a panel in the Museo Correr in Venice, depicts the saint's last rites, with the lion at his bedside (fig.32). All of these pictures are by the same hand, and the architectural elements in the panels in the Brera

and the Correr are very similar to those in the Lindsay panel. There is a prima facie case for supposing that they belong to a single series, but the precise format and nature of such a series – arguably a dossal – is difficult to establish, especially as the panels vary in size and format. Whereas both the Brera panels and the Correr panel have an arched top, the panel in Turin has a flat top. The present panel, on the other hand, is of oblong format with a flat top and does not appear to have been substantially cut down. There is still insufficient evidence to reconstruct these panels into a single complex with any confidence, and, with the exception of the two in the Brera which entered the museum as early as 1820, even their nineteenth-century provenance is obscure.

It has, however, been demonstrated that these panels have a direct connection with a monastic order dedicated to St Jerome called the Gesuati, for monks wearing their habit appear in all of the scenes. This order was founded in the fourteenth century by the Blessed Giovanni Colombini of Siena (died 1367), and was suppressed in 1668.[2] Two of its principal churches were San Girolamo in Siena, and Santa Bunda outside the city walls, but the most likely source for the paintings is the Oratorio di San Girolamo at Ferrara, which was founded in 1424 by Giovanni Tavelli da Tossignano.

The attribution of the present panel and related works is problematic. They have been ascribed in the past to the Sienese painter Guidoccio Cozzarelli (1450–1516/17),[3] but more recent opinion favours an artist of Ferrarese origin working around 1450-5, which would tally well with their probable Ferrarese origin.[4]

Fig.32 · Master of the Gesuati
(active mid-fifteenth century)
The Death of St Jerome
Museo Correr, Venice

1. See Bisogni, 1972, pp.69–79; Milan, 1991, pp.278–83, cat.nos.72 a-e, figs.306–10 (entry by D. Benati).

2. Bisogni, 1972, pp.70–2. Information on the Gesuati also provided by Larry Kanter in a letter to the owner.

3. Van Marle, XVI, p.384; Berenson, 1968, I, p.98.

4. See Milan, 1991, esp. pp.279–82.

10

ATTRIBUTED TO GIOVANNI DI SER
GIOVANNI, CALLED LO SCHEGGIA
1406–1486

[A] The Journey of the Queen of Sheba

Panel, 41.7 × 142.3 cm

[B] The Meeting of Solomon and the Queen of Sheba

Panel, 42 × 141.7 cm

Inscribed on labels on the reverse of each panel: *Carlo Crivelli proveniente della Eccelentissima Casa Litta.*

PROVENANCE: Thomas Blayds; his sale, Christie's, London, 30 March 1849 (lots 161 and 162), as by Crivelli; bought for Lord Lindsay.

EXHIBITION: London, 1893, cat.nos.151 and 161, as Florentine School, *c*.1485.

PRIVATE COLLECTION

These two panels originally decorated the fronts of a pair of *cassoni* (wedding chests). The story of the Queen of Sheba travelling from afar to benefit from the wisdom of King Solomon is related in the Old Testament (Kings 1, and 2 Chronicles 9). The subject became popular in Florence following the meeting of the Eastern and Western churches at the Council of Florence in 1439. It was shown by Lorenzo Ghiberti in one of the scenes on the bronze doors known as the 'Gates of Paradise' for the Florence Baptistery (completed in 1452), which were a lasting source of inspiration for decorative painters. The story readily transferred to the context of a marriage chest. In the first panel, the Queen of Sheba's journey is depicted as a festive procession, and would have been understood as symbolic of a bride coming to her bridegroom in ceremonial mode. In the second panel, the meeting is depicted off-centre, with a group of the king's courtiers and priests to the right, and the queen's retinue and empty carriage occupying the larger left portion of the panel. This scene

was intended to suggest the bride submitting to the wisdom of her husband.[1]

The principal Florentine workshop for *cassoni* was that of Apollonio di Giovanni, who worked in partnership with Marco del Buono Giamberti. They also produced panels for insertion into the ceiling and walls of domestic rooms, and these are frequently confused with *cassone* panels. Many of Apollonio's original designs were repeated by his assistants, who also had access to a studio model-book. The panels exhibited here do not depend directly on models by Apollonio, but the distinctive punching of the gold does appear to originate from his workshop, which suggests that the artist responsible for them may have worked under Apollonio, or at least have had close contacts with him.[2]

Recently an attribution to Giovanni di Ser Giovanni, called lo Scheggia, has been proposed.[3] The younger brother of Masaccio, Scheggia is perhaps best known for the birth salver (*desco da parto*) of *The Triumph of Fame*, honouring the birth of Lorenzo de' Medici in 1449, which was

recently acquired by the Metropolitan Museum of Art, New York.[4] He also painted *cassoni* and other furniture pieces, including the *Adimari Cassone* in the Accademia, Florence,[5] and a *Triumph of a Roman General* in the National Gallery of Scotland.[6]

1. Callmann, 1974, p.43.

2. See Schubring, 1915, cat.nos.196–7, as by the Cassone Master; Berenson, 1963, I, p.17, as by Apollonio di Giovanni; Callmann, 1974, pp.32, 65, pls. 151–2.

3. Letter of 30 April 2000 from Everett Fahy. For the artist, see, most recently, San Giovanni Valdarno, Casa di Masaccio, *Il Fratello di Masaccio: Giovanni di Ser Giovanni detto lo Scheggia*, exhibition catalogue edited by L. Cavazzini, 1999.

4. Formerly in the collection of the New York Historical Society, by whom sold at Sotheby's, New York, 12 January 1995 (lot 69), where acquired by the Metropolitan Museum.

5. See Berenson, 1963, II, pl.733.

6. See H. Brigstocke, 1993, pp.96–7, as by the Master of the Adimari Cassone.

Cat. no. 10 [B]

11

ATTRIBUTED TO GIULIANO AMIDEI
active 1446(?) – died 1496

The Death of St Ephraim and other Scenes from the Lives of the Hermits

Referred to in the discussion below as 'the larger Lindsay panel'

Panel, 80.2 × 228.5 cm

PROVENANCE: Either: William Spence, Florence; from whom bought by Lord Lindsay in 1856, as by 'Laurati' (alias Ambrogio Lorenzetti). Or: Lombardi-Baldi collection, Florence (no.10 in the 1845 catalogue, as 'A. Laurati, Les Anachorètes dans la Thébaïde'); bought by Lord Lindsay through their executor, Ludovico Metzger, on 17 January 1865.

EXHIBITION: London, 1893, cat.no.79, as by Ambrogio Lorenzetti.

PRIVATE COLLECTION

12

FLORENTINE SCHOOL
c.1480–1500

The Death of St Ephraim and other Scenes from the Lives of the Hermits

Referred to in the discussion below as 'the smaller Lindsay panel'

Panel, 49.5 × 163.5 cm

PROVENANCE: See cat.no.11

EXHIBITIONS: London, 1893, cat.no.78, as by Ambrogio Lorenzetti; London, 1904, cat.no.16.

PRIVATE COLLECTION
On loan to the National Gallery of Scotland since 1980

These two panels, focused on the scene of the death of St Ephraim, are inspired by the tradition of Byzantine Thebaids. The earliest surviving visual evidence of this tradition is the late thirteenth-century triptych attributed to Grifo di Tancredi, which was also in Lord Lindsay's collection (cat.no.1), and which is almost certainly based on a lost Byzantine prototype. In fourteenth- and fifteenth-century Italian examples, including the two panels exhibited here, a horizontal format was adopted and new scenes were added, based on a quite different iconographical tradition of Italian origin, which is best illustrated by the fourteenth-century frescoes of eremitical life attributed to Buffalmacco at the Campo Santo in Pisa.[1] These additional scenes were not exclusively of hermits from the Egyptian desert, and the paintings should therefore not, strictly speaking, be described as Thebaids. Indeed, there appears to have been a conscious attempt to update the imagery. St Benedict (died 547), for example, is prominently represented in

both pictures, and not all the new incidents can be identified in the *Vitas Patrum* or the *Lausiac History* by Palladius (for which see cat.no.1). The earliest known example of the fusion of these two traditions is a late fourteenth-century panel of horizontal format from the circle of Mariotto di Nardo. This has been dismembered and the principal parts divided between the Keresztény Museum at Esztergom and a private collection.[2] The division of the panel took place at exactly the spot where the two iconographical traditions met. A copy of the whole picture is in the Uffizi, once attributed to the young Fra Angelico, and currently to an anonymous Florentine master working in the first quarter of the fifteenth century (fig.33).[3] The link between the Uffizi panel and the Campo Santo frescoes was recognized by both Rio and Lord Lindsay.[4] Lindsay's scholarly and empathetic description of the Uffizi picture and his elucidation of its subject-matter vividly conveys the reason why he would have collected all these pictures of monastic life.

The ultimate source of this latter composition may have been a fresco or major painting that is now lost. Its influence was considerable, and it served as the prototype for three further panels, all dating from the fifteenth century – the two presented here, and a third, now dismembered and divided between the National Gallery of Scotland, which has the focal scene of the *Death of St Ephraim* (fig.34), Christ Church Picture Gallery in Oxford, the Jarves Collection at Yale, and the Kunsthaus in Zurich.[5] In the larger Lindsay panel many additional scenes, not present in the Grifo di Tancredi triptych, can be identified: St Benedict (top centre), in his inaccessible cave, receives food from the monks above in a bucket lowered by a rope; the Abbâ Nopi is shown living in a tree trunk; down on the Nile, St Helenus crosses the river on the back of a crocodile; to the right, on the shore, Abbâ Moses, the Indian, is assaulted by the devil for his charity in drawing water for the older hermits (in the Christ Church panel he draws water from a well). Above,

Palladius and the interpreter Theodore talk with John of Lycus at the window of his cell, which he opened only on Saturdays and Sundays.

The smaller Lindsay panel appears to be a little later in date, to judge from the more sophisticated early Renaissance-style architecture. The landscape is less arid, and there are several groups of secular travellers, dressed in red, including, in the lower right corner, a group of horsemen confronted by three skeletons, two in coffins and one standing, motifs reminiscent of the fresco of *The Triumph of Death* in the Campo Santo, Pisa.[6] Just behind, to the right, the same travellers are seen again putting on hermits' habits provided by St Macarius, who urges them to think of death. Here, too, further scenes from eremitical life were added. St Benedict appears twice at the left, receiving his food on the end of a rope, which a devil attempts to sever; and again lying naked in a bed of thorns. Immediately above, Abbâ Macarius converses with a skull; Abbâ Pachomius receives a message from an angel; St Zosimus

finds St Mary of Egypt. Just below, St Paul is buried in a grave dug by lions; and lower still, St Macarius meets the Devil in the form of a woman with hanging bottles. Towards the centre, above the church, Sts Anthony and Paul the Hermit share a loaf provided by an angel; Paul appears again perched in the palm tree nearby; the saint behind appears to be John the Baptist; below him, to the right, St Francis receives the stigmata; to his right there is a hermit asleep in his cell with two kneeling figures with flames rising from their hair; below, to the left, St Paphnutius rids himself of temptation from a scarlet lady; while to the right, the Virgin in a blaze of light appears to St Bernard. In the bottom left corner, St Jerome prays before a crucifix, while his lion fends off a snake; he is shown again nearby removing the thorn from the lion's foot. On the Nile, a naked child in a boat (possibly the soul of a bishop) is tortured by devils; St Helenus recurs, riding the crocodile; and St Maurus saves St Placidus from drowning. Above there is a striking

Fig.33 · Florentine School, early fifteenth century
The Death of St Ephraim and other Scenes from the Lives of the Hermits
Galleria degli Uffizi, Florence

scene of a group of flagellants not found in any of the other panels discussed here.[7]

The issues surrounding the attribution of the two Lindsay panels and the dismembered panel of which the National Gallery of Scotland's *Death of St Ephraim* formed part have never been fully resolved. All three pictures have much in common, not only in general subject-matter and the duplication of specific incidents but also in details of rocks and plants, animals and birds. The Edinburgh *Death of St Ephraim* and the associated fragments, and the larger of the Lindsay panels, appear to be slightly less advanced in style than the more accomplished smaller Lindsay panel, with its more elaborate architecture, landscape and trees. The Edinburgh panel has been attributed to Giuliano Amidei, a Camaldolese monk first recorded in Florence in 1446 at the monastery of San Benedetto fuori di Porta a Pinti. He was later Abbot of Santa Maria di Agnano in the diocese of Arezzo, and is also known to have worked in Rome around 1467–72, and again in 1495. He died in Lucca in 1496.[8]

Amidei's artistic personality has been defined on the basis of a triptych of the *Virgin and Child with Two Angels and Sts Martin, Benedict, Romuald and Michael* in the parish church at Tifi, near Caprese, not far from Sansepolcro and Arezzo. On the basis of comparison with this work, the predella of Piero della Francesca's *Madonna della Misericordia* altarpiece (Museo Civico, Sansepolcro) has also been attributed to Amidei, working perhaps under Piero's supervision. The Tifi altarpiece depicts no rocks or plants to assist stylistic comparison with the Sansepolcro predella, the Edinburgh fragment, and the larger Lindsay panel, and the figures there are much larger in scale. Yet there is a distinct similarity between all four works in the facial types, staring

eyes, and the handling of hair and beards, and it seems reasonable to place them together, tentatively, under the name of Giuliano Amidei. The Sansepolcro altarpiece was commissioned in 1445, but completed only some fifteen years later, and there is some evidence that the Tifi altarpiece was painted around 1480. If they are indeed by Amidei, the larger Lindsay panel and the Edinburgh *Death of St Ephraim* might possibly date from between 1460 and 1480.

The smaller Lindsay panel was probably painted towards the end of the century by an artist familiar with the works attributed to Amidei.[9] It shows some stylistic affinity with artists in the circle of Paolo Uccello, and may be compared in particular with a picture of *Scenes of Monastic Life and the Vision of St Bernard* in the Accademia, Florence, where one finds a very similar group of flagellants around a crucifix. Other secular figures in the Accademia picture recall the horsemen in the foreground of the smaller Lindsay panel. The artist responsible for the Accademia picture has not been convincingly identified, although the name of Giovanni di Francesco has been proposed.[10]

Fig.34 · Attributed to Giuliano Amidei (active 1446–died 1496)
The Death of St Ephraim
National Gallery of Scotland, Edinburgh

1. See Bellosi, 1974, pl.4.
2. Sold at Christie's, London, 28 June 1974 (lot 47), from a Scottish private collection, where it had been since 1863. It was previously in the collections of E. Joly de Bammeville and the Revd Walter Davenport Bromley, for whom see pp.28, 33, nn. 9 and 10 in this catalogue. See H. Brigstocke, 'Panels showing the "Death of St Ephraim"' in *Burlington Magazine*, CXVIII, 1976, pp.585–9; E. Callmann, 'Thebaid Studies' in *Antichità Viva*, XIV, 3, 1975, pp.3–22, nn.27 and 28.
3. See L. Berti et al. (eds.), *Gli Uffizi: Catalogo generale*, Florence, 1979, p.487.
4. Rio, 1836, pp.52 ff.; Lindsay, 1847, III, pp.57–64.
5. See E. Callmann 'A Quattrocento Jigsaw Puzzle' in *Burlington Magazine*, XCIX, 1957, pp.153 ff. (where the two Lindsay panels are confused, and the larger picture reproduced with the measurements of the smaller one). See also J. Byam Shaw, *Paintings by Old Masters at Christ Church*, Oxford, 1967, pp.40–4; Lugano, Museo Cantonale d'Arte, *Manifestatori delle cose miracolose*, exhibition catalogue by G. Freuler, 1991, pp.250–2, cat.no.98; Brigstocke, 1993, pp.17–19.
6. Bellosi, 1974, pl.20.
7. The subject-matter of this panel is discussed in detail by R. Langton Douglas in London, 1904, pp.52–4.
8. For Amidei, see M. Salmi, 'Piero della Francesca and Giuliano Amidei' in *Rivista d'Arte*, XXIV, 1942, pp.26–44.
9. Everett Fahy has recently proposed (letter of 30 April 2000) that both Lindsay panels may be by Amidei.
10. Berenson, 1963, p.87, pl.693.

13

TUSCAN SCHOOL
mid-fifteenth century

Madonna and Child with a Goldfinch

Panel, 76.8 × 50.6 cm (original panel); 67.2 × 41.6 cm (painted surface)

The frame is probably nineteenth century, but corresponds closely to the size of the original.

Inscribed on an old label on the reverse: *A. Vivarini.*

PROVENANCE: Thomas Blayds; his sale, Christie's, London, 30 March 1849 (lot 115), as by A. Vivarini; bought by Lord Lindsay.

PRIVATE COLLECTION

According to legend, the goldfinch acquired the red spot on its brow when it removed a thorn from Christ's head during his ascent to Calvary, and was splashed with a drop of blood. Its inclusion in images of the Madonna and Child is, therefore, a symbol of Christ's future Passion.

This well-preserved panel was acquired as the work of Antonio Vivarini, a Venetian artist who had some influence on Girolamo di Giovanni da Camerino, to whom this picture was subsequently attributed.[1] Girolamo di Giovanni was the leading representative of a tradition of painting in the Marches which had absorbed a range of influences both from northern Italy (especially Venetian and Paduan artists such as Giovanni Boccati, the Vivarini, Crivelli and Mantegna) and from the Tuscan and Umbrian followers of Benozzo Gozzoli and Piero della Francesca. However, the Lindsay panel differs from Girolamo's *Madonna and Child Enthroned* in the Cini Collection, Venice, where the balance of Venetian and Tuscan stylistic influences is far subtler and more assured (fig.35).[2] It may more meaningfully be compared with the work of an anonymous Tuscan artist active around 1460, dubbed the 'Honolulu Master' after a painting of *The Virgin with the Blessing Christ Child* in the Honolulu Academy of Arts.[3] This little known picture has a similar elegantly incised and painted background of gold brocade, and the figures share some of the same distinctive facial features of the Virgin and Child in the Lindsay panel, such as the tight lips, vacant eyes and prominent ears.

It has been suggested that the Honolulu Master may have worked in the valley of the Arno west of Florence, and that he was close to another anonymous artistic personality, the Master of Fucecchio. This artist, named after an altarpiece of *The Virgin and Child in Glory with Sts Sebastian and Lazarus, Mary Magdalene and Martha* at

Fucecchio, near Empoli, has been identified elsewhere as Giovanni di Ser Giovanni, called lo Scheggia, to whom Lindsay's cassone panels of *Solomon and the Queen of Sheba* have also recently been attributed (see cat.no.10).[4] Clearly the present picture is not by the same hand, and is arguably more accomplished in technique. It appears to be by a Tuscan artist close to Domenico Veneziano and Giovanni di Francesco.

Fig.35 · Girolamo di Giovanni da Camerino (active 1449–1473)
Madonna and Child Enthroned
Cini Collection, Venice

1. Berenson, 1968, p.193, as studio of Girolamo di Giovanni da Camerino; P. Zampetti, *Paintings from the Marches*, London, 1971, p.92, as workshop of Giovanni da Camerino.

2. For the Cini picture and for a useful discussion of the artist, see F. Zeri *Due dipinti, la filologia e un nome ...*, Turin, 1961, p.78.

3. F. Zeri 'Seven centuries of Italian Art' in *Apollo*, CIX, 1979, pp.88–9, fig 5. I am indebted to Everett Fahy for suggesting this connection.

4. San Miniato, Museo Diocesano, *Mostra d'arte sacra della diocesi di San Miniato*, exhibition catalogue by L. Bellosi, 1969, pp.56–7, cat.no.42. See also Berenson, 1963, II, pl.723.

14

PSEUDO PIER FRANCESCO FIORENTINO
active mid-fifteenth century

The Madonna and Child with a Goldfinch

Panel, 68 × 50 cm (including the engaged frame)

PROVENANCE: M. Vicard (possibly Jean-Baptiste Wicar), according to the 1849 Christie's sale catalogue; Thomas Blayds; his sale, Christie's, London, 30 March 1849 (lot 118), as by Lippo Dalmasio; bought for Lord Lindsay.

PRIVATE COLLECTION

The figures in this picture are based on the design of a *Madonna and Child* by Francesco Pesellino (*c.*1422–1457) in the Isabella Stewart Gardner Museum, Boston, of which there is another version in the Keresztény Museum, Ezstergom. Two other versions of the present picture, both attributed to the Pseudo Pier Francesco Fiorentino and both featuring the distinctive rose-hedge background, are at the University of Santa Barbara, California, and the Walters Art Gallery, Baltimore.

The attributional history of this group of works is complex. The present picture was first attributed to Pier Francesco Fiorentino by Van Marle, who initiated the confusion by defining this artist's oeuvre around the picture in Boston mentioned above.[1] Bernard Berenson subsequently renamed the artist responsible for these works the 'Pseudo Pier Francesco Fiorentino', to distinguish him from the mediocre Pier Francesco Fiorentino (1444/5 – after 1497), whose manner can be gauged from three firmly attributed works. Berenson defined his Pseudo Pier Francesco as 'a craftsman of considerable skill, particularly as a flower painter, who made a business of copying and piecing together figures from Fra Filippo, Pesellino and their followers'.[2] However, it is now clear that the pictures grouped under this name are not all the work of a single artist, but rather the products of a busy Florentine workshop active over several decades in the second half of the fifteenth century, and specialising in popular but essentially mechanical derivations from designs by Fra Filippo Lippi and Pesellino. As Federico Zeri has observed, 'the group of Lippesque-Pesellinesque panels is characterised by a solid technique of impeccable precision, and by a mechanical derivation from specific models which apart from some very rare instances are either by Filippo Lippi or Pesellino'.[3]

1. Van Marle, XIII, p.455, as by Pier Francesco Fiorentino or an artist in his circle.

2. Berenson, 1963, I, p.171.

3. F. Zeri, *Italian Paintings in the Walters Art Gallery, Baltimore*, Baltimore, 1976, I, pp.80–1.

15

ATTRIBUTED TO
DOMENICO GHIRLANDAIO
1448/9–1494

St Barbara Crushing her Infidel Father, with a Kneeling Donor

Panel, 68.1 × 47.4 cm

Inscribed on an old label on the back: *St Barbara standing beside her tower by Domenico Ghirlandajo the first teacher of Michael Angelo [...] 1480*

PROVENANCE: Conte delle Bordille, from whom acquired by William Spence, Florence; from whom bought by Lord Lindsay on 6 May 1856, as by Benozzo Gozzoli.

EXHIBITION: London, 1893, cat.no.88, as school of Pollaiuolo.

PRIVATE COLLECTION

The legend of St Barbara was introduced into Italian art from the East and is recounted in *The Golden Legend* of Jacopo da Voragine. Barbara's father, Dioscurus of Heliopolis, shut her in a tower for protection from the eyes of men. While away, he arranged for architects to construct for her a splendid bathroom. At her request they added a third window in order to reflect the Trinity and the three sources of light for the Christian soul. Barbara then baptised herself in the bathroom's sanctified water. However, her anti-Christian father ordered her to worship pagan gods instead, and when she refused he pursued her to her rural hiding-place and cut off her head. The story is described in detail both by Lord Lindsay in his *Sketches* (I, p.cxcii) and by Mrs Jameson in her widely read *Sacred and Legendary Art* of 1848 (II, pp.103–12). One of the earliest representations of the story is an eighth-century fresco at Santa Maria Antiqua, Rome. However, it was only in the second half of the fifteenth century that the cult gathered momentum in Italy. One of the earliest Florentine representations was painted in 1468–9 by Cosimo Rosselli in an altarpiece for the Compagnia di Santa Barbara in the church of Santissima Annunziata in Florence (now in the Galleria dell'Accademia there).[1]

In the present picture, St Barbara holds a model of the tower and stands triumphant over the body of her father. Her martyrdom is shown as a separate incident in the left background. Although unidentified, it seems likely that the young donor in this painting may have been a member of the Compagnia di Santa Barbara at Santissima Annunziata, or of some similar confraternity dedicated to her. The painting was acquired by Lord Lindsay as by Benozzo Gozzoli (1420–97), and was subsequently attributed to Bastiano Mainardi (1466–1513), a pupil and later brother-in-law of Domenico Ghirlandaio.[2]

More recently, it has been proposed that the painting might be an early work by Domenico Ghirlandaio himself, datable to around 1470–5,[3] and convincing parallels can indeed be made with other early works by him. For example, there is a close formal connection between the present painting and Ghirlandaio's frescoed *St Barbara* in the church of Sant'Andrea at Cercina, near Florence, which is considered by most recent scholars to be among his earliest extant works (fig.36).[4] The saint is there shown in a similar perpendicular pose, holding a tower, and crushing her father underfoot. His foreshortened pose is almost identical in the two works, and St Barbara's physiognomy and the distinctive rendition of her

hands are also very similar. The latter features recur in some of Ghirlandaio's early panel paintings, such as the *Virgin and Child Enthroned with Sts Catherine, Stephen, Lawrence and Dorothy* of *c*.1478–9 (Museo Nazionale di San Matteo, Pisa),[5] and the celebrated altarpiece in the Uffizi of the *Virgin and Child Enthroned with Sts Michael, Justus, Zanobius and Raphael, and Four Angels*, which has been variously dated to the 1470s or the early 1480s.[6] The handling of St Barbara's red mantle in the Lindsay panel, with its clearly visible underdrawing, is especially close to that of the Archangel Raphael's cloak and to the cope of St Justus in the latter altarpiece. Finally, the distinctive wispy clouds in the Lindsay panel also feature in other works by Ghirlandaio, including the Pisa altarpiece mentioned already, and the fresco of *The Exequies of Santa Fina* (*c*.1473–5) in the Collegiata at San Gimignano.[7] It is difficult to find direct parallels for the distinctive coastal landscape among Ghirlandaio's earliest works, but similar vistas appear in several of his frescoed scenes in the Tornabuoni Chapel in Santa Maria Novella, Florence (1486–90).

It seems likely, then, that this *St Barbara* is the earliest panel painting by Domenico Ghirlandaio to have been identified, executed perhaps in the early to mid-1470s, not long after he left the workshop of his probable master, Alesso Baldovinetti (1425–1499). As such, it is a work of considerable interest for our understanding of the artistic formation of an artist who went on to run one of the most successful workshops in late fifteenth-century Florence.

Fig.36 · Domenico Ghirlandaio (1448/9–1494)
St Barbara
Sant'Andrea, Cercina (Florence)

1. See A. Padoa Rizzo, 'La Cappella della Compagnia di Santa Barbara della "Nazione Tedesca" alla Santissima Annunziata di Firenze nel Secolo XV. Cosimo Rosselli e la sua "Impresa" Artistica' in *Antichità Viva*, XXVI, 3, 1987, pp.3–18.

2. Van Marle, XIII, p.224; Berenson, 1963, I, p.125.

3. Suggested independently by Lisa Venturini, who dates the picture to *c*.1475 (letter of 26 February 2000) and Everett Fahy (letter of 30 April 2000), who dates it to *c*.1470. It is, however, hard to reconcile the style of this picture with that of the *Ruskin Madonna* in the National Gallery of Scotland, for which Fahy has also proposed an attribution to Domenico Ghirlandaio, *c*.1470 (see Brigstocke, 1993, pp.202, 204 n.29).

4. See, most recently, Kecks, 1998, pp.36–8.

5. Kecks, 1998, pp.84–5.

6. Kecks, 1998, pp.117–21.

7. Kecks, 1998, pp.50–7.

16

JACOPO DEL SELLAIO
(JACOPO DI ARCANGELO DI JACOPO)
c.1441–1493

St Jerome in the Wilderness with St Mary of Egypt, and the Young Christ Blessing St John the Baptist

Panel, 61.8 × 87.8 cm

PROVENANCE: Lombardi-Baldi collection, Florence; bought through their executor, Ludovico Metzger, by Lord Lindsay on 17 January 1865, with an attribution to Andrea del Castagno.

PRIVATE COLLECTION

St Jerome (c. 342–420), a scholar from Dalmatia who preferred Plato to the prophets, dreamed that he had been summoned before the judgement seat of God and condemned as a Ciceronian and a false Christian. He submitted himself to four years of solitude and penance in the Egyptian desert, and his struggles against temptations of the flesh are narrated in his epistle to Eustochium. Lord Lindsay cites a long extract from this epistle in the *Sketches* (p.clxviii).

St Jerome, his arms outstretched in rapturous adoration of a crucifix, is shown at the centre with his traditional attributes – a cardinal's hat, a skull, the rock of self-punishment in his hand, and a lion, an allusion to the occasion when he assisted a wounded lion by drawing a thorn from its paw (see also cat.no.9). St Mary of Egypt (died 433), another hermit saint, is shown at the right in a cave. She lived in penance in the desert beyond the River Jordan, growing her hair to cover her body. At the left, the adolescent St John the Baptist, who spent much of his life in the wilderness, receives the blessing of a similarly youthful Christ, an iconographically unusual episode.

The picture was acquired as by Andrea del Castagno, but it is in fact a characteristic mature work by Jacopo del Sellaio.[1] Sellaio's distinctive, dry tempera technique, his sharp linear modelling and his predilection for light-toned pastel colouring reflects the influence of Botticelli; according to Vasari, the two artists may have studied together under Filippo Lippi. Sellaio painted several other pictures of *St Jerome in the Wilderness* alone (Nationalmuseum, Stockholm; Contessa Rasini, Milan; and formerly Berlin, Kaiser Friedrich Museum (destroyed)).[2] They are all set against highly imaginative panoramic landscapes which offer an idyllic foil to the arid desert foregrounds with their highly stylised trees and fantastic, almost surreal, rocky shelters.

1. Berenson, 1963, I, p.196.
2. Berenson, *ibid.* See further N. Pons 'Una provenienza per Jacopo del Sellaio' in *Antichita Viva*, XXXIII, 6, 1994, pp.16–19.

17

ATTRIBUTED TO
JACOPO DEL SELLAIO (JACOPO DI
ARCANGELO DI JACOPO)
c.1441–1493

Scenes from the Life of Virginia
Panel, 39.9 × 166.2 cm

The Death of Lucretia
Panel 39.9 × 166.2 cm

PROVENANCE: Said to be from the Lombardi-
Baldi collection, Florence (but not included in the
1845 catalogue of the collection); bought by Lord
Lindsay from Ludovico Metzger, through the
Florentine dealer Torello Bacci, on 17 January
1865.

EXHIBITION: London, Royal Academy, *Winter
Exhibition*, 1871, cat.nos.271–2, as by Filippino
Lippi.

PRIVATE COLLECTION

Fig.37 · Attributed to Filippino Lippi (c.1457–1504)
Scenes from the Life of Virginia
Musée du Louvre, Paris

Fig.38 · Attributed to Filippino Lippi (c.1457–1504)
The Death of Lucretia
Galleria Palatina, Palazzo Pitti, Florence

1. H. Horne, *Botticelli*, Princeton 1979 ed., pp.283–6.

2. Berenson, 1963, p.108, as Filippino Lippi; R. Lightbown, *Botticelli*, 2 vols., London, 1978, p.105; Florence, 1992, pp.241–3, cat.no.9.5, as Filippino Lippi (entry by J. Nelson).

3. A. Scharf, *Filippino Lippi*, Vienna 1935, pp.117–18, cat.nos.153–4, as studio of Filippino Lippi; Berenson, 1963, p.108, as early Filippino Lippi; Florence, 1992, p.242–3, as Jacopo del Sellaio, an attribution also endorsed by Everett Fahy.

4. See Florence, 1992, pp.238–9, cat.nos.9.1 and 9.2 (entries by N. Pons).

5. See J.W. Goodison and G. Robertson, *Fitzwilliam Museum, Cambridge, Catalogue of Paintings: Volume II, Italian Schools*, Cambridge, 1967, pp.153–6, cat.no.M.75.

Although panels of this kind were also used as bed-heads or were set into a *spalliera* or wainscot, the physical evidence indicates that these two panels were originally the front panels from a pair of *cassoni* (marriage chests). The Virginia panel has signs of lock marks at the top left and top right, as well as a mark from some central attachment. The Lucretia panel shows no signs of lock marks or of gouges for keys, but has evidently had some attachment in the centre.

The story of Virginia, from Roman history, is told by Livy (*History of Rome*, III, 44–51) and Valerius Maximus (De Pudicitia, VI, 1), as an example of the virtue of chaste modesty. In the first incident, represented on the left, Marcus Claudius, servant of Appius Claudius, chief of the Decemvirs, seizes Virginia on the pretext that she is his slave, and was stolen from his house as a small girl. A bystander to the right remonstrates. In the central scene, set within a Florentine Renaissance-style basilica, Virginia is led before a tribunal. Appius Claudius presides, surrounded by courtiers and seated on a raised throne, and he finds in favour of Marcus Claudius. Icilius, to whom Virginia is betrothed, prevents Marcus Claudius from seizing her. Virginia's father Virginius turns away, having approached the judge without success. In the next scene, on the right, Virginius, having secured a delay so that Virginia's nurse can be called as a witness, attempts to take her life to protect her virtue before escaping on one of the waiting horses.

The story of Lucretia, who was raped by Sextus Tarquinius at Collatia, is also told by Livy (*History* of Rome, I, 57–60) and Valerius Maximus (*Facta et dicta memorabilia*), who both link it with the story of Virginia. In the first scene, on the left, Lucretia, having been raped, collapses in the presence of her husband Tarquinius Collantius, her father Spurius Lucretius, Publius Valerius, whom Livy records as accompanying Lucretius from Rome after he had received his daughter's summons, and Brutus. In the central scene the body of Lucretia, who stabbed herself, is laid out in the forum and Brutus, standing in front of a column, calls on the people for vengeance. The horseman on the right may be Sextus Tarquinius, with the single companion demanded by Livy's account.

The most celebrated pairing of these two scenes in Florentine art is by Botticelli, in panels now in the Accademia Carrara, Bergamo (Virginia), and the Isabella Stewart Gardner Museum, Boston (Lucretia).[1] These, however, did not provide the prototype for the present pictures, since they are clearly later in date, probably c.1499. Another pairing of these two scenes is to be found in panels now divided between the Louvre, Paris (fig.37) and the Palazzo Pitti, Florence (fig.38). Sometimes attributed to Filippino Lippi, they may date from about 1483–90. It has been argued, but not conclusively, that they may depend on some earlier design by Botticelli.[2] The attempt to unify the sequence of events through the architecture, and the relationship between these elements and the landscape beyond, suggest the combined influence of Filippo Lippi and Botticelli. These pictures are close in both composition and style to the Lindsay pictures, which have likewise been attributed traditionally to Filippino Lippi. Nevertheless, the Lindsay pictures appear to be by a different hand, possibly Jacopo del Sellaio.[3] A series of *spalliera* panels with *Scenes from the Story of Esther*, attributed to Jacopo del Sellaio, show close stylistic affinities to the present panels.[4] Many of Jacopo del Sellaio's works dating from the 1470s and 1480s show Botticelli as a source of inspiration. He was at his best when painting secular scenes for domestic furniture, such as the *cassone* panel with the *Story of Cupid and Psyche* in the Fitzwilliam Museum, Cambridge, where his elegant, linear technique and sinuous modelling of form are fully in evidence.[5]

SANDRO BOTTICELLI AND WORKSHOP
1444/5–1510

St Lawrence with a Female Donor

Panel, 131 × 83.8 cm

The frame, excluding the base, appears to be nineteenth century.

Inscribed on the base of the frame: VRSVLA PS PERIGORI FECIT FIER … Inscribed on a label on the reverse: 1886. March 15 no 76.

PROVENANCE: Unknown, but probably acquired by Lord Lindsay (or just possibly by Anne Lindsay) in Florence, where Félicie de Fauveau made a watercolour copy of the head in an album of copies she bequeathed to Lord Lindsay in 1878.

PRIVATE COLLECTION

St Lawrence (died 258) was ordained deacon by Pope Sixtus II. After the pope was imprisoned by the prefect Decius for failing to give up the treasures of the church, he instructed Lawrence to distribute them instead to the poor. Given three days notice to give up the treasures, Lawrence presented Decius with a motley collection of the poor, sick and maimed, informing him that these were the riches he had promised to yield. He was condemned to be roasted alive on a gridiron and is usually represented in paintings with this attribute. In the *Sketches*, Lord Lindsay cites an account of this scene written by Prudentius towards the end of the fourth century.[1] The image of St Lawrence, dressed as a deacon, acquired the status of an icon or devotional image in fifteenth-century Italy and the present picture, with a kneeling nun of the Ursuline order, accords with this tradition. A celebrated narrative cycle of the life of St Lawrence was painted by Fra Angelico in the late 1440s for the principal chapel of Pope Nicholas V in the Vatican.

The attribution of this picture to Botticelli and his studio is relatively recent.[2] Although the somewhat stiff modelling and static posture of the saint might indeed suggest the involvement of a workshop assistant, this little known picture perhaps deserves more favourable attention than it has received. The possibility that it is an autograph work by Botticelli himself, perhaps dating from about 1490, when the artist entered a conservative and retardataire phase, with simpler forms and more abstract and internalised emotions, cannot be excluded.[3]

Lindsay's acquisition of this somewhat introspective religious image by Botticelli is of particular interest to anyone concerned with analysing the roots of his artistic tastes. Although A.F. Rio, in his *De La Poésie Chrétienne*,[4] had written with rapture about Botticelli's paintings on the side walls of the Sistine Chapel, for their synthesis of epic and pastoral poetic themes – especially the scene of *Moses and the Daughters of Jethro* – Lindsay had done little more than pay lip-service to these frescoes when he saw them in the spring of 1842. Yet he was one of the first British collectors to buy a Botticelli painting – anticipated only by William Young Ottley, who bought the *Mystic Nativity* now in the National Gallery, London, in 1799; Lord Northwick, who had bought the Botticelli *Portrait of a Young Man*, also in the National Gallery, by 1804 (wrongly attributed to Masaccio) and, in 1846, *The Virgin Adoring the Sleeping Christ Child* recently purchased by the National Gallery of Scotland (fig.17); and William Coningham, who owned the *tondo* of the *Adoration of the Kings* (National Gallery, London), wrongly attributed to Filippino Lippi, at the time of his sale in 1849. The cult of Botticelli, associated with the aesthetic movement, was in effect launched by Walter Pater's essay on the artist (1873), which celebrated the duality of Christianity and Paganism in the work of an artist who wrote a commentary on Dante and became a disciple of Savanorola. Pater, with great empathy, conveys the 'sentiment with which he [Botticelli] infuses his profane and sacred persons, comely, and in a certain sense like angels, but with a sense of displacement or loss about them – the wistfulness of exiles conscious of a passion and energy greater then any known issue of them explains, which runs through all his varied work with a sentiment of ineffable melancholy'.[5]

1. Lindsay, 1847, III, pp.179–80.
2. Berenson, 1932, p.106, as Botticelli studio; *idem*,1963, p.33, as Botticelli, but heavily restored.
3. R. Lightbown, *Botticelli*, 2 vols., London 1978, p.158, cat.no.16.
4. Rio, 1836, p.129.
5. W. Pater, *Studies in the History of the Renaissance*, London, 1873, p.44. See further M. Levey, 'Botticelli and Nineteenth-Century England' in *Journal of the Warburg and Courtauld Institutes*, XXIII, 1960, pp.291–306.

19

FRANCESCO BOTTICINI (FRANCESCO
DI GIOVANNI DI DOMENICO)
1446–1497

The Virgin and Child Enthroned with St Francis, the Donor Agnoletta Benvenuti, the Archangel Raphael and Tobias

Panel, 149.3 × 169.8 cm

PROVENANCE: Benvenuti (later Rinuccini) Chapel, Church of San Pier Scheraggio, Florence; Palazzo Rinuccini, Florence; William Spence; from whom acquired by Lord Lindsay on 6 May 1856 for 700 francs.

EXHIBITION: London, Royal Academy, 1878, *Winter Exhibition of Works by the Old Masters and by Deceased Masters of the British School*, cat.no.220, as by Cosimo Rosselli.

PRIVATE COLLECTION
On loan to the National Gallery of Scotland since 1988

NOTE: This entry presents a summary of the author's researches on Botticini's altarpiece and its provenance which will be published in full in her forthcoming article, 'Ancora su Francesco Botticini' in *Paragone* (in press).

1. See Brigstocke, 1982, p.304, n.3.

2. F. Fantozzi, *Nuova guida ovvero descrizione storico-artistico-critica della città e contorni di Firenze*, Florence, 1842, p.742; *Catalogo dei quadri ed altri oggetti della Galleria Rinuccini*, Florence, 1845, p.16, no.45.

3. For the painting see L. Venturini, *Francesco Botticini*, Florence, 1994, pp.67, 116, cat.no.42 (with full bibliography). A. Padoa Rizzo, 'Per Francesco Botticini' in *Antichità Viva*, XV, 5, 1976, p.9, suggested that the altarpiece was partly executed by Botticini's workshop.

4. G. Richa, *Notizie storiche delle chiese fiorentine divise ne' suoi quartieri*, Florence, 1754–62, IV (1755), p.16. San Pier Scheraggio, one of the most ancient churches in Florence, was incorporated by Vasari in the sixteenth century into the fabric of the new Uffizi, although worship continued there until the end of the eighteenth century.

5. V. Follini and M. Rastrelli, *Firenze antica e moderna illustrata*, Florence, 1789–1802, V (1794), pp.132–3. The painting is mentioned as a lost work by W. and E. Paatz, *Die Kirchen von Florenz*, Frankfurt am Main, IV, 1952, p.676, n.38.

6. The relevant documents will be published in full in my forthcoming article, mentioned above.

The son of a painter of playing cards, Botticini was apprenticed in 1459 to the successful Florentine painter Neri di Bicci (1418–1492). From 1471 he was a member of the Confraternity of the Archangel Raphael at Santo Spirito, and in 1472 he was inscribed in the Confraternity of St Luke, the painters' guild. Botticini's youthful works belong to the mid-fifteenth-century pictorial tradition running from Domenico Veneziano to Alesso Baldovinetti. The early 1470s saw a decisive shift towards the manner of Verrocchio, as exemplified by such works as the *Madonna and Child Enthroned with Saints* of 1471 (Musée Jacquemart-André, Paris), and the altarpiece of *The Three Archangels* (Uffizi, Florence), in which, however, the influence of his contemporary Botticelli is also apparent. The grandiose *Coronation of the Virgin* (National Gallery, London) was painted in the mid-1470s for the humanist Matteo Palmieri, who also commissioned Botticini to illuminate a poem (the *Città di Vita*, now in the Biblioteca Medicea Laurenziana, Florence). Noteworthy among his mature works are two large tabernacles in the museum at Empoli; the *Madonna in Glory* in the Louvre; a *Pietà* in the Musée Jacquemart-André; and the *Madonna Enthroned with Saints* in the Metropolitan Museum of Art, New York.

When Lord Lindsay bought the present altarpiece from William Spence in 1856, it was said to have come from the Palazzo Rinuccini.[1] It is, in fact, mentioned in the palace in Fantozzi's 1842 guide-book to Florence, and is then listed, as anonymous 'Florentine School', in a catalogue of the Rinuccini collection published in 1845.[2] The attribution to Botticini first advanced by Berenson in 1900 has not been challenged.[3]

Recent research by the present writer into chapels in Florentine churches under Rinuccini patronage has led to the identification of this altarpiece with one described in 1755 by Richa in the Church of San Pier Scheraggio: 'There follows the third chapel, belonging to the Marchese Rinuccini, which was originally [under the patronage] of the Benvenuti family ..., and in the painting Filippo Lippi painted Mary, St Francis, the Archangel Raphael and a kneeling female saint, in whom he portrayed Agnoletta Benvenuti'.[4] A later guide of 1794 reiterates the iconography of the altarpiece, the name of the praying donor, and the attribution to Lippi.[5]

Further archival research has brought to light some biographical details about the donor, Agnoletta Benvenuti. [6] Born in 1442, she was the wife of Alessandro Del Rosso Pieri (born 1428), a hide and leather worker ('galigaio'). The couple, who were childless, lived in the Santa Croce quarter of Florence, precisely in the parish of San Pier Scheraggio, which was the funerary church of the Del Rosso Pieri family. Alessandro died some time between 1495 and 1501, but Agnoletta was still alive in 1507. It is unclear why she should have been portrayed in the painting without her husband, occupying the position to the Virgin's right usually reserved for men. Agnoletta may have commissioned the painting after her husband's death, in which case it would be one of Botticini's last works, since the artist himself died in July 1497. Certain stylistic affinities with the altarpiece of *The Penitent St Jerome with Four Saints*, painted for Girolamo Rucellai around 1495 (now in the National Gallery, London), lend some support for this hypothesis. This late date for the altarpiece would also accord better with the donor's apparent age than the previously proposed one of around 1480.

The saints in the painting have no direct connection with the dedication of the church, nor with the baptismal names of members of the Benvenuti or Del Rosso Pieri families. In view of her rather severe habit, with veil and wimple, and the obvious protection afforded to her by St Francis, one might tentatively suggest that Agnoletta Benvenuti may have been a lay devotee ('pinzochera') of the convent of Franciscan tertiaries dedicated to the Archangel Raphael, which in the fifteenth century was located at the fringe of the Santa Croce quarter, beyond what was then called the Porta della Giustizia.

LISA VENTURINI

20

MASTER OF SANTO SPIRITO
active late fifteenth and early sixteenth centuries

The Virgin and Child with Sts John the Baptist and Verdiana

Panel, 154.3 × 152 cm. The frame is nineteenth century.

PROVENANCE: William Spence, Florence, 1860 (visible in a painting of his Gallery in the Palazzo Giugni, possibly by Spence himself, in a private collection);[1] from whom bought by Lord Lindsay (unusually, the date of acquisition is recorded neither in the Lindsay nor the Spence archives).

PRIVATE COLLECTION

St Verdiana (died 1222 or 1242), who was a lay recluse, is the patron saint of the town of Castelfiorentino outside Florence. She made a pilgrimage to Rome and on returning home entered a cell where she was molested by serpents, but where she remained until her death. She is generally represented in painting as a middle-aged nun with two snakes and a basket, as in the present picture. There is a church in Florence dedicated to her, but no evidence as yet to connect this altarpiece with that church.

The Master of Santo Spirito, to whom this picture is convincingly attributed,[2] was a Florentine painter active towards the end of the fifteenth century, who is named after the three important altarpieces he executed for the church of Santo Spirito, including a *Trinity* in the Corbelli chapel, which dates from the last decade of the century. Earlier he had painted a *Virgin Adoring the Christ Child* as part of Baldovinetti's *Tabernacle of the Holy Sacrament* in Sant' Ambrogio, Florence, for which payment was received in 1484-5. It has been claimed that this distinctive artist may be identified as Giovanni di Michele da Larciano, called il Graffione, whom Vasari describes in the first edition of his *Lives of the Artists*.[3] An alternative suggestion, which is now widely but not universally accepted, is that the Master of Santo Spirito's paintings were produced in the joint workshop of Donnino di Domenico di Donnino del Mazziere (1460–after 1515) and his brother Agnolo di Domenico (1466–1513).[4]

1. J. Fleming, 'Art Dealing and the Risorgimento: III' in *Burlington Magazine*, CXXI, 1979, p.510, nn. 13–14; E. Callmann, 'William Spence and the transformation of Renaissance cassoni' in *Burlington Magazine*, CXLI, 1999, p.336, fig.14.

2. F. Zeri, 'Eccentrici fiorentini' in *Bolletino d'arte*, XLVII, 1962, p.236 n.2; E. Fahy *Some Followers of Domenico Ghirlandaio*, New York, 1976, p.192.

3. For the artist and documents relating to him, see H. Horne, 'Il Graffione' in *Burlington Magazine*, VIII, 1905, pp.189–96; C. Gamba in *L'Arte*, LVI, 1957, p.111; and Zeri, 1962 (*loc. cit.* above), pp.216–36.

4. A. Padoa Rizzo, 'Agnolo di Donnino: Nuovi Documenti: le fonti e la possibile identificazione con il Maestro di Santo Spirito' in *Rivista d'Arte*, 40, 1988, pp.125–68 (I am indebted to Everett Fahy for this reference); see also A. Padoa Rizzo, 'I del Mazziere' in Florence, 1992, pp.114–15.

21

MATTEO DI GIOVANNI
active 1452–died 1495

Sts Agatha and Lucy

Panel, 58.5 × 33.8 cm; painted surface: 54.1 × 31.2 cm
Two separate panels, possibly originally the lateral
sections of a triptych, which were joined together in
the nineteenth century within a new architectural
framework. The figures are of different height, and
stand on different floors, but have similar tooling in
their haloes.

PROVENANCE: Bought by Lord Lindsay in Rome
in 1842.

PRIVATE COLLECTION

St Agatha and St Lucy were two of the early
Christian martyrs. Agatha (died 251), from
Catania in Sicily, had her breasts cut off during
her martyrdom and is depicted carrying them on
a plate. She was visited by St Peter and was made
whole and well again. St Lucy (died 303), a virgin
of Syracuse in Sicily, had been with her sick
mother to pray at the tomb of St Agatha, who
appeared to her in a vision and told her to protect
the city of Syracuse as she herself had protected
Catania. Lucy is usually depicted carrying her
eyes on a plate; the loss of her eyes during martyrdom is not a feature of the early legends and
may be interpreted metaphorically as an expression of her name – *lucia* or light. The best account
of these legends in Lord Lindsay's day appeared in
Mrs Jameson's *Sacred and Legendary Art* (II, pp.229–
37). That the grisly attributes of the two saints
were meant to be understood symbolically is
confirmed in the present panel, where there
appear to be three or four breasts on Agatha's
plate, and at least half a dozen eyes on Lucy's.

This panel, which is clearly Sienese in origin,
has been attributed both to Matteo di Giovanni
and to Guidoccio Cozzarelli (1450–1516/17), who
probably trained under Matteo around 1470.[1]
Matteo di Giovanni is first recorded working in
Siena Cathedral, and his earliest altarpiece, now
in the Museo dell' Opera del Duomo, dates from
1460. Cozzarelli has usually been regarded as an
uninspired follower of Matteo, but this is contra-
dicted by his two altarpieces in the church of San
Bernardino in Sinalunga, dating from c.1483 and
c.1486. Thus, it has been noted that 'many of
Matteo's late works, in which the nervous
draftsmanship and bright palette of his earlier
pictures are relaxed, have often been assigned to
Cozzarelli while some of Cozzarelli's best paintings are still taken for Matteo's'.[2] On balance the
present painting, with its well-drawn and
carefully modelled figures, seems closer to
Matteo di Giovanni; the figures may be compared, for instance, with figures in his St Barbara
altarpiece, signed and dated 1478, in San
Domenico, Siena.

A notable technical feature of this panel is the
delicate handling of St Agatha's red dress, which
has been painted over the gold ground.

1. Berenson, 1932, p.158, as by Cozzarelli; *idem*, 1968, I,
    p.257, as by Matteo di Giovanni; Van Marle, XVI, p.358,
    as near Neroccio di Landi.

2. K. Christiansen in New York, 1988, p.282. For the
    relationship between these two artists, see also B.
    Berenson, *Essays in the study of Sienese painting*, 1918.

22

ATTRIBUTED TO
BENVENUTO DI GIOVANNI
1436 – after 1518

The Meeting of Jephthah and his Daughter

Panel, 36.1 × 82.3 cm (cut down at the left)

PROVENANCE: Thomas Blayds; his sale, Christie's, London, 30 March 1849 (lot 108), as by Andrea Orcagna; bought by Harris for Lord Lindsay.

EXHIBITION: London, 1893, cat.no.128, as Florentine School.

PRIVATE COLLECTION

1. Berenson, 1932, p.456; L. Kanter in New York, 1988, p.345, as an early work.

2. Van Marle, XVI, pp.518–19, as follower of Francesco di Giorgio.

3. Schubring, 1915, cat.no.479.

4. This attribution was suggested recently by Keith Christiansen (verbal communication).

The Old Testament warrior Jephthah, who had successfully commanded the Israelites against the Ammonites, had promised God that if he won he would sacrifice 'the first creature that comes out of the door of my house to meet me when I return'. This panel shows his only daughter, Iphis, and her maidens stepping forward to welcome him on his arrival, thus sealing her fate. Jephthah, on a black horse, clutches his breast in despair. The soldiers wave olive branches to symbolise the peace that will follow their victory, while Iphis similarly offers an olive branch to the captive moor. The story is told in Judges 11: 30–40.

This decorative panel might have formed part of the furnishings of a domestic interior. Within the city walls in the background there are elaborately drawn buildings in classical style. The artist has bravely attempted in the courses of bricks to explore three-dimensional space by means of linear perspective. The picture surface is notable for the virtuosity of the tooling and punching of the men's armour and the ladies' golden dresses. The soldiers' armour was originally silvered to enhance the glittering surface, but this has subsequently tarnished and darkened.

Although acquired by Lord Lindsay as a Florentine work, this panel is almost certainly of Sienese origin, but there has been little consensus about its precise attribution. The names of various artists have been suggested, including Pietro di Domenico,[1] Francesco di Giorgio,[2] and Girolamo di Benvenuto.[3] Perhaps the most plausible attribution is to Benvenuto di Giovanni, who may have trained under Vecchietta, and who in his early years was also influenced by Matteo di Giovanni, Francesco di Giorgio and Neroccio de' Landi.[4] Benvenuto di Giovanni's style changed considerably in the 1480s and the present picture would have been painted early in his career, around 1470, while he was still combining ideas and motifs from a wide range of sources.

23

PIETRO DI DOMENICO
1457–1501(?)

The Madonna and Child with Sts Sebastian and Jerome

Panel, 64.2 × 39.6 cm

The engaged frame probably dates from the nineteenth century, but is evidently of the same proportions as the original.

PROVENANCE: Acquired by Colonel James Lindsay (Lord Lindsay's cousin) before 1847;[1] thence by inheritance.

EXHIBITION: London, 1904, cat.no.48, as by Pietro di Domenico.

PRIVATE COLLECTION

St Sebastian (died 288) was the saint most frequently invoked against the plague. The Emperor Diocletian had condemned him to death for proclaiming his Christian beliefs. Although shot by arrows (a traditional emblem of plague and pestilence), he survived but was later clubbed to death. He was buried in the catacombs at the feet of Sts Peter and Paul. (For the story of St Jerome, see under cat.no.9).

This exceptionally well-preserved panel has been attributed to the Sienese painter Pietro di Domenico for all of its known history.[2] The artist may have trained under Benvenuto di Giovanni (see previous entry) and was influenced by Matteo di Giovanni and Francesco di Giorgio. Pietro di Domenico's career is poorly documented. His best known works, which may date from relatively late in his career, after he had fallen under the influence of Signorelli and Pietro Orioli, include a signed *Madonna and Child with Sts Jerome and John the Baptist* at York City Art Gallery, and a signed *Nativity with Sts Martin and Galganus* in the Pinacoteca at Siena. The present picture may also have been painted towards the very end of the fifteenth century.

The 'graceful decorative quality' which has been noted as a typical feature of the artist's later works is brilliantly reflected in the present picture, especially in the elaborate and meticulous tooling of the Virgin's dress.[3] Bold incisions in the gesso suggest the use of a cartoon for the design of the figures.

1. See Lindsay, 1847, III, p.97.
2. See Berenson, 1968, I, p.343.
3. L. Kanter in New York, 1988, p.345.

24

LUCA SIGNORELLI
c.1450–1523

Scenes from the Lives of Sts Joachim and Anne

Panel, 23.5 × 43 cm (X-rays indicate that the original paint surface terminates about 1.5 cm from the top of the panel)

The Birth of the Virgin

Panel; 23.5 × 43 cm (X-rays indicate that the original paint surface terminates about 1.5 cm from the top of the panel)

PROVENANCE: Thomas Blayds; his sale, Christie's, London, 30 March 1849 (lot 81), bought by Harris for Lord Lindsay.

EXHIBITIONS: London, Burlington Fine Arts Club, *The Work of Luca Signorelli and his School*, 1893, cat.nos.3 and 4; London, 1893, cat.nos.143 and 145; London, 1930, cat.nos.248 and 249; Cortona and Florence, *Mostra di Luca Signorelli*, 1953, cat.nos.11 and 12; Manchester, City Art Gallery, *European Old Masters*, 1957, cat.nos.9 and 12; London, Wildenstein and Co., *The Art of Painting in Florence and Siena from 1250 to 1500*, 1965, cat.nos.73–4; London, National Gallery, *Signorelli in British Collections*, 1998, cat.nos.7–8.

PRIVATE COLLECTION

1. A detailed account of these legends is provided by A. Jameson, *Legends of the Madonna*, 1852, pp.149–59. The subject of the second panel was first correctly identified by M. Crutwell, *Signorelli*, London, 1899, p.131.

2. Letters from Laurence B. Kanter to the present owner (14 June 1984) and to the present writer (16 February 2000).

3. R. Fry, 'The Umbrian Exhibition at the Burlington Fine Arts Club' in *Burlington Magazine*, XVI, 1909–10, p.273.

4. Berenson, 1932, p.531; Berenson, 1968, I, p.395.

5. For the best account of this issue, and indeed of all the issues surrounding these panels, see London, National Gallery, *Signorelli in British Collections*, exhibition catalogue by T. Henry, 1998–9, p.12, cat.nos.7–8.

6. Letter to Anne Lindsay, dated 28 March 1842.

These are two panels from a predella that would almost certainly have been entirely devoted to scenes from the life of the Virgin. In the first panel Joachim, husband of Anne and father of the Virgin, according to the second-century apocryphal Gospel of James, is shown three times in separate episodes: his expulsion from the temple by the high priest Issacher because he had not fathered a son or daughter in Israel; his retreat to the country where he fasted for forty days and avoided his barren wife, until an angel visited him and comforted him with promises; and his reunion with his wife Anne at the Golden Gate, which preceded the conception of the Virgin Mary. All of these stories, which traditionally precede any representation in art of the life of the Virgin (although St Bernard had objected to the invocation of saints who had lived before Christ except as historical figures) can be found in *The Golden Legend* of Jacopo da Voragine.

The second panel would appear to represent the *Birth of the Virgin*, although it was identified as the *Birth of St John the Baptist* when Lord Lindsay acquired it in 1849, a title which had still not been corrected at the time of its exhibiton at the Burlington Fine Arts Club in 1893. Signorelli's depiction of Joachim as a figure writing by the bedside explains the iconographical confusion, for he more readily suggests the figure of Zacharias in scenes of the birth and naming of St John. Signorelli's own panel of this subject in the Louvre, which predates the Lindsay panels, shows Zacharias in this way.[1] It has been suggested that two further panels by Signorelli (divided in 1922) representing *The Presentation of the Virgin in the Temple* (Richmond Museum of Fine Arts, Virginia) and *The Marriage of the Virgin* (National Gallery of Art, Washington) might also have belonged to the same predella,[2] but the technical evidence to confirm this match is inconclusive.

The Lindsay panels were acquired as by Signorelli. Although, curiously, the renowned critic Roger Fry doubted this attribution, it has otherwise been widely accepted and is no longer an issue.[3] The question of their date and place in Signorelli's development is more problematic. Signorelli began his career at Cortona and then worked in the Sistine Chapel at the Vatican in 1481–2. His earliest altarpiece, a *Virgin and Child with Saints* at Perugia, dates from 1484, and by 1493–8 he was working at Città di Castello, where he painted three successful altarpieces. Then, from 1499–1503, he was employed at the Cathedral of Orvieto on frescoes in the chapel of San Brizio, including the celebrated scenes of *The End of the World*, a cataclysmic vision of nude forms and humanised demons.

Bernard Berenson believed Lindsay's panels to be early works, but a date around 1490 or a little later seems most likely.[4] This issue affects speculation as to which Signorelli altarpiece might have stood above this predella. *The Adoration of the Magi*, painted for the church of Sant'Agostino in Città di Castello in 1493–4 and now in the Louvre, and the 'Belladonna Altarpiece' of 1491 at Volterra, have been proposed as possibilities.[5] The very unusual lighting in the Louvre picture, with the source of light coming from behind and casting deep shadows out of the picture, is similar to that in the Lindsay panels.

Lindsay's acquisition of these Signorelli panels, as well as a *Madonna and Child with Saints* by him now in the National Gallery of Art in Washington (see fig.22), is of particular interest in the light of his ambivalent if predictable response to Signorelli's frescoes at Orvieto, which he saw in January 1842. At that time he wrote:

'It is impossible to estimate his merit without visiting Orvieto – his works in the Sistine Chapel are inferior to these, and his oil paintings with two or three exceptions, very poor. His distinguishing merit in the eyes of the historian of art is his having preceded Michael Angelo in anatomy etc. and doubtless he did much in that line and Michael Angelo profited by studying him. But some of these frescoes are very beautiful in other respects. The Antichrist for instance, one of the earlier I should think, as there are no muscular exhibitions in it, is a grand moral composition, full of character and expression; and in the Glory of the Blessed, meeting in Paradise and crowned by angels, the composition is peculiarly symmetrical and graceful. On the other hand he has drawn his naked figures scrupulously from the models, which were not always very select ones; there is thus a sad want of grace – his men and women are clumsily built, fat often as porpoises – the attitudes are contorted and twisted in every direction in order to exhibit his powers in foreshortening etc. and in his efforts to be expressive he often runs into caricature. Moreover he marks the muscles so strongly that they are unnaturally in action. Still, as first attempts in this line, they are excellent and interesting, and altogether mind and feeling predominate throughout his compositions.'[6]

Presumably the panels exhibited here, with their simple narrative and restrained design, would also have been acquired for their expressive conjunction of mind and sentiment.

25

BERNARDINO PINTURICCHIO
c.1452–1513

The Virgin and Child with
Two Angels

Panel, 128 × 83.1 cm

PROVENANCE: Marchesa Frescobaldi, Florence; bought by Lord Lindsay in 1865.

EXHIBITIONS: London, Royal Academy, *Winter Exhibition*, 1878, cat.no.198; London, 1930, cat.no.259; Manchester, City Art Gallery, *European Old Masters*, 1957, cat.no.12.

PRIVATE COLLECTION

The representation of the Virgin Mary with one breast exposed and about to suckle the Christ Child (known in Italian as the 'Madonna del latte') is of ancient origin and was quite common in the Renaissance, but was condemned for its nudity at the Council of Trent (ended 1564). A small figure of the penitent St Jerome is visible in the left background of the painting.

Acquired as by Pinturicchio and since then invariably accepted as by him, with possible assistance from his studio.[1] It has been suggested that Giovanni Battista Caporali (c.1475–c.1555) of Perugia, who collaborated with Pinturicchio on an altarpiece of *The Coronation of the Virgin* in the Pinacoteca Vaticana, may have worked on the execution of the present picture, but from a cartoon by Pinturicchio.[2] Alternatively, it may well be a relatively late work by Pinturicchio himself.

Pinturicchio, who was born in Perugia, had begun as a follower of Perugino and collaborated with him at the Sistine Chapel in Rome in 1481–2. This influence, as well as that of the young Raphael, is still discernible in the present picture, which was almost certainly painted after Pinturicchio had returned to Perugia in 1495, and quite possibly after he had settled in Siena in 1504. The landscape of rolling hills and tall wispy trees reflects the artist's Umbrian origins. The figure of the Virgin is similar to the equivalent figure in the Santa Maria degli Angeli polyptych, now in the Galleria Nazionale dell'Umbria in Perugia.[3]

1. C. Ricci, *Pintoricchio*, London, 1892, pp.145–8; Berenson, 1968, I, p.344, as a studio work; F. Todini, *La Pittura Umbra dal Duecento al primo Cinquecento*, 2 vols., Milan, 1989, I, pp.290–1, as a studio work; F. Nucciarelli, *Studi sul Pinturicchio dalle prime prove alla Cappella Sistina*, 1998, p.283, as an autograph late work.

2. This idea was first proposed by Francis Russell.

3. See F. Santi, *Galleria Nazionale dell'Umbria: Dipinti, sculture e oggetti dei secoli XV–XVI*, Rome, 1985, pp.91–4, cat.no.77.

26

MATTEO BALDUCCI
active 1509–1555

Diana and Actaeon

Panel, 57 cm diameter

PROVENANCE: Torello Bacci, Florence; from whom bought by Lord Lindsay in January 1865.

EXHIBITIONS: London, 1904, cat.no.59; London, 1930, cat.no.956.

PRIVATE COLLECTION

This panel was probably a birth salver or *desco da parto*, a tray used for carrying gifts to a woman who had given birth. The story is from Ovid's *Metamorphoses* (III: 138–253). Actaeon, out hunting, surprises Diana, chaste goddess of the moon and the hunt, and her nymphs, while they are bathing. She transforms him into a stag and he is attacked by his own hounds. In the present picture, Diana is shown splashing water over the stag's back. Such mildly erotic mythological subjects were regularly depicted in paintings destined for domestic interiors.

Matteo Balducci was an Umbrian artist from the circle of Pinturicchio. He may have been involved with Pinturicchio in the decoration of the ceiling of the Piccolomini Library in the Cathedral at Siena, and there are paintings by him in the art galleries at Siena and Gubbio. However, he remains a shadowy artistic personality.

The present picture is a distinctive and amusing rendition of the story, and is clearly the work of a talented decorative painter with a penchant for landscape. It has been compared with a series of circular panels representing the *Seasons* in a private collection, also attributed to Balducci, where one finds similar facial types and landscape.[1] The group of Diana and the bathing nymphs is a witty adaptation of the celebrated antique *Three Graces*, which was already displayed in the Piccolomini Library in Balducci's day.

1. J.A. Crowe and G.B. Cavalcaselle, *A History of Painting in Italy,* edited by T. Borenius, 1914, V, pp.420–1. See further T. Borenius, 'Unpublished Cassone Panels' in *Burlington Magazine*, XLI, 1922, pp.18–21; Berenson, 1968, I, p.24.

27

NORTH ITALIAN
early sixteenth century

Portrait of a Young Woman

Panel, 57.2 × 43.9 cm (whole panel); 47 × 33.7 cm (painted surface). The panel is unusually thick (3 cm).

PROVENANCE: Possibly identical with the painting attributed to Ridolfo Ghirlandaio which Lord Lindsay bought from the Palazzo Riccardi, Florence, at an unknown date.

EXHIBITION: London, 1893, cat.no.159, as by Ridolfo Ghirlandaio.

PRIVATE COLLECTION

The sitter holds a jewel in her left hand in the form of a flaming cornucopia, a symbol of Hymen, god of marriage.[1] Similar motifs flank the pendant jewel suspended from her pearl necklace. It seems likely, therefore, that this may be a betrothal or marriage portrait, but the identity of the sitter is unknown.

Acquired as by the Tuscan painter Ridolfo Ghirlandaio (1483–1561), this portrait was subsequently attributed by Bernard Berenson to the Venetian Vittore Carpaccio (1460/6–1525/6).[2] Although the Carpaccio attribution has been questioned[3] – and the picture is even ignored completely in more recent literature devoted to the artist[4] – no convincing alternative has been proposed.

Carpaccio was described by Vasari as a portrait painter and other contemporary sources refer to portraits by him of eminent men and women. Although no portraits of standard bust length have been identified, Carpaccio's well characterised heads in his celebrated narrative cycles – for instance the *Departure of St Ursula* in the Accademia, Venice – demonstrate his capacity in this genre. Furthermore, he painted one striking full-length *Portrait of a Young Knight* against a landscape background (Museo Thyssen-Bornemisza, Madrid), which dates from about 1510.[5] Unfortunately, none of the documentary or visual evidence throws much positive light on the problems surrounding the present picture, which is both more robust and intimate in character than one would expect of Carpaccio. It therefore seems more likely that the artist responsible for this picture originated from some other North Italian city, perhaps Bologna or Ferrara, or even Mantua.

1. This was kindly pointed out by Diana Scarisbrick.
2. Berenson, 1894, p.101; *idem*, 1932, p.135; *idem*, 1957, I, p.57, as Carpaccio. See also J.P. Richter in *Repertorium für Kunstwissenschaft*, XVII, 1894, p.242, as Carpaccio.
3. T. Borenius, 'Two Unknown Carpaccios' in *Burlington Magazine*, XXIII, 1913, p.127, who questioned the attribution to Carpaccio.
4. See, for example, J. Lauts, *Carpaccio*, London, 1962, where it is not even mentioned among the rejected works.
5. For a discussion of Carpaccio as a portrait painter, see P. Humfrey in *Dictionary of Art*, 1996, 5, pp.821–2.

28

THE MASTER OF THE EMBROIDERED FOLIAGE
active in Brussels in the late fifteenth century

The Virgin and Child

Panel, 90.5 × 76.5 cm (cut down at the top)

Bears false date and signature at centre left: 1513 AD [in monogram]

PROVENANCE: Dr Frederick Campe; his sale, Christie's, London, 13 May 1849 (lot 35), as by Dürer; bought by Lord Lindsay for 40 guineas.

EXHIBITIONS: London, Burlington Fine Arts Club, *Exhibition of Pictures by Masters of the Netherlandish and Allied Schools of XV or early XVI Centuries*, 1892, cat.no.46, as by school of Geeraert David; London, New Gallery, 1899, cat.no.85; Bruges, *Exposition des Primitifs Flamands et d'Art ancien*, 1902, cat.no.132, as anonymous.

PRIVATE COLLECTION
On loan to the National Gallery of Scotland since 1995

The name given to the anonymous but gifted Netherlandish painter known as the Master of the Embroidered Foliage is based on his characteristic foregrounds, carpeted with flowers and decorative leaves executed with a meticulous technique of tiny dots of paint used to realise the minutiae of textures and surfaces, almost as if depicted in needlepoint. His treatment of landscape is equally distinctive, with trees arranged in ordered lines and characterised by stylised foliage. He appears to have been active in Brussels and the South Netherlands, and was clearly influenced by such Flemish masters as Rogier van der Weyden, especially in his treatment of the Virgin and Child, and by Hugo van der Goes. The present picture is one of several autograph variant versions of this composition and is distinguished by the throne with its elaborate gold-embroidered damask.[1] A picture in the Groeningen Museum, Bruges, has a similar throne and a wall separating the landscape background, with the added feature of two angels crowning the Virgin.[2] Other versions, such as a painting in a private collection, Amsterdam, and the centrepiece of a triptych at Lille, have a more elaborate open landscape, without a throne or wall to obstruct the view.[3]

1. Friedländer, 1969, p.83, no.84c, pl.79; E. du Callatay, 'Etude sur le Maître au feuillage en broderie', in *Bulletin des Musées Royaux des Beaux-Arts de Belgique*, 1972, 1, 4, pp.17ff.

2. Friedländer, 1969, p.83, no.84b.

3. Friedländer, 1969, pp.82–3, nos.84a–b.

29

LUCAS CRANACH THE ELDER
1472–1553

An Allegory of Melancholy

Panel, 113 × 72.4 cm

Signed with the artist's dragon cipher, inscribed MELENCOLIA, and dated 1528 on the central ledge. The panel has been cut down, especially along the right hand edge, with the loss of the seated figure's wings.

PROVENANCE: Dr Frederick Campe; his sale Christie's, London, 13 May 1849 (lot 40); bought by Lord Lindsay for 27 guineas.

EXHIBITIONS: London, Burlington Fine Arts Club, *Exhibition of Early German Art*, 1906, cat.no.43; London, Grosvenor Gallery, 1913, cat.no.41; Basel, 1974, cat.no.171.

PRIVATE COLLECTION
On loan to the National Gallery of Scotland since 1993

The iconography and imagery of the present picture are strongly influenced by Dürer's celebrated engraving of *Melencolia*, dated 1514 (fig.39).[1] The meanings of Dürer's print have been widely debated. It has been shown that it is based on a passage in Agrippa's *De occulta philosophia*, which was first printed in 1533, but was apparently available to Dürer in manuscript from 1510. According to Galenic psychology, which was followed throughout the medieval period, all men could be classified under four temperaments: sanguine, choleric, phlegmatic and melancholic. These corresponded to four elements or four planets. Melancholy was associated with earth and with Saturn, and is characterised as earthy, pensive and condemned to menial occupations. Thus, in Dürer's print, the figure of Melancholy holds compasses for measuring and artisan's tools lie neglected on the ground. In Cranach's painting, too, she is surrounded by a sphere, compass, gimlet and chisel. However, another line of thought regarded melancholy as the highest humour, associated with the frenzy of genius. This theory of melancholy originates in a pseudo-Aristotelian text which was disseminated by the Renaissance writer Marsilio Ficino in *De triplici vita*, and it has been argued that Dürer was aware of Ficinian theory. At this point scholars divide over whether the figure of Melancholy in Dürer's print is suffering from the frustration of a thwarted genius – the figure's wings folded and inactive, the tools neglected – or whether on the other hand she is in a creative visionary trance, inspired by Saturn and the angel of Saturn, and protected from demonic dangers.

In the present picture Cranach radically changes the meaning of Dürer's concept. The woman is depicted as lost in a trance while children play, but she is inspired not by Saturn but by Satan and this is underlined explicitly by the witches' sabbath – devil worship – which Cranach includes in the upper left portion of his picture. The seated woman is sharpening or peeling a stick – possibly a magic wand. The picture reflects Martin Luther's belief that melancholy was a moral issue, far removed from the humanistic preoccupations of Dürer. Cranach then developed this concept in a sequence of related paintings that move still further away from Dürer's imagery, towards a more emphatic preoccupation with the imagery of witchcraft. Three of these, all of them dated 1532, are in the Unterdenlinden Museum, Colmar, the Statens Museum in Copenhagen,

and (this one horizontal in format) in a private collection, Sweden. A copy of the present picture, providing evidence of the losses on the right-hand edge noted above, is at Columbus (Ohio).[2]

As court painter to Frederick the Wise of Saxony at Wittenberg from 1504, Cranach was to find himself at the hub of the Protestant Reformation. Cranach and Luther became close friends, the artist made numerous portraits of the religious leader, and as the present picture apparently indicates, absorbed some of his ideas.

Fig.39 · Albrecht Dürer (1471–1528)
Melencolia
British Museum, London

1. The best account of the iconography of Dürer's print and Cranach's paintings is F. Yates, *The Occult Philosophy in the Elizabethan Age*, 1979, pp.49–59. See further Basel, 1974, I, pp.292–3, cat.nos.171–3.

2. For the sequence of Cranach's paintings, see C. Heck 'Entre humanisme et réforme: la Mélancolie de Lucas Cranach l'Ancien' in *Revue du Louvre et des Musées de France*, 1968, pp.257–65.

30

ATTRIBUTED TO BERNARDINO LANINO
1509/13 – after 1581

St John the Baptist in the Wilderness

Panel, 23.9 × 23.9 cm

PROVENANCE: Marchesa Castellani, Turin; bought by
Lord Lindsay through William Spence, Florence, on 26
July 1856 for £80, as from the circle of Leonardo da
Vinci.

EXHIBITIONS: London, Burlington Fine Arts Club,
*Catalogue of Pictures by Masters of the Milanese and allied schools
of Lombardy*, 1898, cat.no.62, as by Cesare da Sesto;
London, Grafton Gallery, *Exhibition of Old Masters in aid of
the National Art Collections Fund*, 1911, cat.no.36, as
Milanese School, sixteenth century; London, Royal
Academy, *Leonardo da Vinci*, 1952, cat.no.260, as by Cesare
da Sesto.

PRIVATE COLLECTION
On loan to the National Gallery of Scotland since 1975

1. Berenson, 1968, I, p.87.

2. A. Venturi, 'Esposizione al Burlington Fine Arts Club di
Londra' in *L'Arte*, I, 1898, p.318; G. Frizzoni, 'Appunti
critici intorno alle opere di pittura delle scuole italiane
nella Galleria del Louvre' in *L'Arte*, IX, 1906, pp.411–12;
Berenson, 1907, p.242; Berenson, 1932, p.278;
G. Romano and A. Quazza, *Bernardino Lanino e il
Cinquecento a Vercelli*, Turin, 1986, p.240; M. Carminati,
Cesare da Sesto, Milan, 1994, p.21, as by Lanino;
G. Romano, 'Bernardino Lanino e il Cinquecento a
Vercelli' in Vercelli, 1995, pp.17–18.

3. C. de Tolnay, 'Quelques dessins inédits de Léonard de
Vinci' in *Raccolta Vinciana*, fasc. XIX, 1962, pp.111–14,
fig.14, as by Leonardo; K. Clark, *Leonardo da Vinci*,
Harmondsworth, 1967, pp.155–6, as by Leonardo;
Vercelli, 1995, p.17, as by Lanino.

4. C. Amoretti, *Memorie storiche sulla vita, gli studi, e le opere di
Leonardo da Vinci*, Milan, 1804, p.157.

5. H. Cook, 'Leonardo da Vinci and some copies' in
Burlington Magazine, XX, 1911, p.129; W. Suida, *Leonardo
und sein Kreis*, Munich, 1929, pp.156–7, 218–19, pl.169.

6. W. Pater, *Studies in the History of the Renaissance*, London,
1873, pp.111–12.

This little panel was acquired by Lord Lindsay
with an attribution to the circle of Leonardo da
Vinci, a view reflected in its subsequent attribution to his Lombard follower, Cesare da Sesto
(1477–1523).[1] An alternative attribution to
Bernardino Lanino, who was closely associated
with Gaudenzio Ferrari at Vercelli before moving
to Lombardy around 1534, has also been proposed
by several scholars.[2] Although in execution the
present picture seems closer to Lanino than to
Cesare da Sesto, the subtlety of its response to
Leonardo, and in particular the imaginative and
delicate treatment of the landscape, surpass
Lanino's normal level. In any case, the original
concept almost certainly derives from Leonardo.
A closely connected red chalk drawing, formerly
at the Museo Baroffio, Varese (stolen and never
recovered), was traditionally attributed to
Leonardo, although more recently it too has been
claimed for Lanino.[3] A seventeenth-century
reference to a picture of *St John the Baptist* 'which
is said to have been painted by Cesare da Sesto
from a cartoon by [Leonardo da] Vinci' ('*che vuolsi
dipinto da Cesare da Sesto sul cartone del Vinci*'), in the
celebrated Litta Visconti collection near Milan,[4]
might conceivably relate to Lord Lindsay's
picture.

A second, larger version of this composition,
now in the Louvre, was already at Fontainebleau
in 1625 attributed to Leonardo da Vinci (it was
altered before 1695 to represent *Bacchus*!). It has
since been attributed to Cesare da Sesto,[5] or to the
school of Leonardo. In his well-known essay,
published in 1873, the aesthete Walter Pater
compared the latter picture to Leonardo's autograph *St John the Baptist*, also in the Louvre, and
vividly conveyed 'the duality of pagan and
Christian impulses in Renaissance art'.

'And these pupils of his acquired his manner
so thoroughly, that though the number of
Lionardo's authentic works is very small indeed,
there is a multitude of other men's pictures
through which we undoubtedly see him, and
come very near to his genius ... [Sometimes] the
original remains, but has been a mere theme or
motive, a type of which the accessories might be
modified or changed; and these variations have
but brought out the more the purpose or expression of the original. It is so with the so-called
Saint John the Baptist of the Louvre, one of the
few naked figures Lionardo painted – whose
delicate brown flesh and woman's hair no one
would go out into the wilderness to seek, and
whose treacherous smile would have us under-
stand something far beyond the outward gesture

or circumstance. But the long reed-like cross in
the hand, which suggests Saint John the Baptist,
becomes faint in a copy at the Ambrosian Library,
and disappears altogether in another in the
Palazzo Rosso at Genoa. Returning from the last
to the original, we are no longer surprised by
Saint John's strange likeness to the Bacchus,
which hangs near it, which set Gautier thinking
of Heine's notion of decayed gods, who, to maintain themselves after the fall of paganism, took
employment in the new religion. We recognise
one of those symbolical inventions in which the
ostensible subject is used, not as matter for
definite pictorial realisation, but as the starting-
point of a train of sentiment, as subtle and vague
as a piece of music. No one ever ruled over his
subject more entirely than Lionardo, or bent it
more dexterously to purely artistic ends. And so it
comes to pass that though he handles sacred
subjects continually, he is the most profane of
painters; the given person or subject, Saint John
in the Desert, or the Virgin on the knees of Saint
Anne, is often merely the pretext for a kind of
work which carries one quite out of the range of
its conventional associations.'[6]

One can only speculate whether this sense of
paradox echoes Lindsay's response at the time he
bought his version, which appears to lie far
outside the normal range of his taste.

31

ITALIAN SCHOOL
mid-sixteenth century

Portrait of a Young Man Tying his Garter

Panel, 89 × 65.8 cm (including additions all sides); 86.4 × 63.3 cm (original panel)

Inscribed on a label on the reverse: *Originale del frate pagato L.180: l'anno 1619. L'anno 1773 il Principe Chigi Romano offeri per questo Quadro il prezzo di L. 1000*

PROVENANCE: Palazzo Monte Catini, Lucca; Principessa Elizabetta Poniatowski (née Monte Catini), from whom bought for £120 by Lord Lindsay's wife, Margaret, on 9 February 1856, through the agency of L.J. Fuller, Florence, as by Sebastiano del Piombo.[1]

PRIVATE COLLECTION
On loan to the National Gallery of Scotland since 1993

Although acquired with an attribution to Sebastiano del Piombo, this striking portrait shows more obvious stylistic affinities with the work of Florentine mannerist painters such as Agnolo Bronzino (1503–1572) and Francesco Salviati (1510–1563). The polished surface, hard modelling of the flesh and metallic sheen of the red sleeve point to this area. Several portrait drawings from the circle of Bronzino and Pontormo, notably one at Chatsworth,[2] have similar seated, *contrapposto* poses and three-quarter length truncated figures. On the other hand, the informality of the characterisation, with the sitter engaged in the mundane (and possibly suggestive) activity of tying his garter, and the treatment of the hands, are untypical of Florentine portraiture of this period, and might suggest a more provincial Tuscan origin (the picture, it may be noted, was acquired in Lucca). It has even been suggested that it might be North Italian or, conceivably, from north of the Alps.

1. Letter of 12 August 1891 to her grandson David (Bal).
2. See M. Jaffé, *The Devonshire Collection of Italian Drawings: Tuscan and Umbrian Schools*, London, 1994, p.84, cat.no.51.

32

FLEMISH SCHOOL
late sixteenth century

Portrait of Giambologna in his Studio

Oil on canvas, 138.8 × 101.8 cm

PROVENANCE: Marchesa Guadagni (died 1864), Florence; William Spence (recorded in a painting, possibly by Spence himself, of his Galleria in the Palazzo Guigni, Florence);[1] from whom bought by Lord Lindsay, c.1864, without attribution.

EXHIBITION: Edinburgh, Royal Scottish Museum, London, Victoria and Albert Museum, Vienna, Kunsthistorisches Museum, *Giambologna: Sculptor to the Medici*, exhibition catalogue edited by C. Avery, 1978-9, cat.no.216, as attributed to Hans von Aachen.

PRIVATE COLLECTION
On loan to the National Gallery of Scotland since 1988

Giambologna (1524-1608) was a Flemish sculptor who travelled to Italy in 1550 and was persuaded to settle in Florence under the patronage of the Medici. He rose to become the dominant sculptor in the city, carving large-scale marble groups and fountains, and he acquired an international reputation through the dissemination of his small bronzes.

The sculptor is here shown seated on a stool at a table, holding a pair of dividers and twisting round to look out at the viewer. In the background there is a view of the artist's studio with a large model of the marble *Neptune* for the *Fountain of Oceanus*, originally in the Amphitheatre of the Boboli Gardens, Florence (later moved to the *Isolotto* at the southern end of the gardens, then transferred to the Bargello and replaced by a copy). The project dates from between 1563 and 1575 and this offers a possible basis for dating the portrait. Even further in the background of the studio, on a three-legged modelling stool, can be made out the figure of *La Fiorenza* (Florence) for another fountain at the Medici villa of Castello outside Florence, but now at the neighbouring Villa Petraia.

The previous attribution of this portrait to Hans von Aachen (1552-1615), which is not convincing on stylistic grounds, was based on a reference by the writer Carel van Mander, who wrote in 1617 that the German artist had visited Florence and named Giambologna as the subject of one of the portraits he painted there.[2] The picture does not appear to be German, nor to be by any of the artists associated with the Court of Rudolf II at Prague; neither is it obviously Italian, although a tentative attribution to the Bolognese Bartolomeo Passarotti has been suggested recently. Its author was in fact almost certainly Flemish. It may be compared generically to portraits by Cornelis Ketel (1548-1616), although it cannot be by Ketel himself, since he did not visit Italy.[3]

1. J. Fleming, 'Art Dealing and the Risorgimento: III' in *Burlington Magazine*, CXXI, 1979, p.570, nn. 13–14; E. Callmann, 'William Spence and the transformation of Renaissance cassoni' in *Burlington Magazine*, CXLI, 1999, p.339, fig.14.

2. C. van Mander, *Het leven der doorluchtighe Nederlandtsche en Hoogduytsche schilders* (1617), edited by H. Floerke, Munich, 1906, II, p.285.

3. I am grateful to Dr Christopher Brown for this generic attribution.

33

ATTRIBUTED TO DOSSO DOSSI
*c.*1490–1541/2

Bacchus (after Titian)

Oil on canvas, 92.5 × 74.5 cm

PROVENANCE: John Rushout, 2nd Baron Northwick,
Thirlestane House, Cheltenham; his sale, Phillips,
Cheltenham, 11 August 1859 (lot 1095); bought Lord
Lindsay, as by Agostino Carracci.

PRIVATE COLLECTION

This is a brilliant copy, with some minor variations in the landscape, of the central figure in
Titian's celebrated *Bacchus and Ariadne* in the
National Gallery, London (fig.40). The original
was completed in 1523 for Alfonso d'Este, Duke of
Ferrara, and was installed in that year in his
studiolo, known as the 'Camerino d'alabastro'
('the little alabaster room'), in the ducal apart-
ments at Ferrara, as part of a series of paintings
with bacchic subjects.[1] It remained there until
appropriated and taken to Rome in 1598 by the
Papal Legate, Cardinal Pietro Aldobrandini, when
the state of Ferrara passed to the papacy.

The present copy was already attributed to
Agostino Carracci (1557–1602) by the German
writer Gustav Waagen in his description of the
pictures at Northwick Park.[2] Agostino had in all
likelihood seen Titian's *Bacchus and Ariadne* when
he worked for the D'Este in the early 1590s,[3] but
this copy appears to belong to an earlier generation. It is, in fact, extremely close in style to the
work of Dosso Dossi, the eccentric court painter
to the D'Este, who had himself contributed
several canvases to the cycle in the Camerino.[4]

The figure of Bacchus corresponds very closely
to Titian's original, although the modelling of
the flesh here is slightly flatter and harder and
his musculature is chunkier, characteristics
which are entirely in keeping with Dosso's
manner. The passages which most clearly reveal
Dosso's hand, however, are those which the
copyist was obliged to invent in the process of
isolating this single figure from its narrative
context, namely the foreground plants and parts
of the landscape. The fantastic, spectral buildings, which seem to float in the mid-distance,
and the distinctive, flecked highlighting of the
trees and the plants in the foreground, find
numerous counterparts in Dosso's paintings.
Arguably the closest parallels are to be found in
his painting of *Apollo* in the Galleria Borghese,
Rome, which has been dated to about 1524.[5] This
would indicate that his copy of *Bacchus* was made
shortly after Titian's painting arrived in Ferrara.
We can only speculate as to whether the copy was
made as a spontaneous response on the part of a
fellow artist to the brilliance of Titian's original,
or – perhaps more likely – as a commission from
some admiring member of the Ferrarese court.

The reasons behind Lindsay's decision to buy
this picture are extremely hard to fathom. He can
hardly have chosen it for its pagan and arguably
its sexually ambiguous subject-matter. His
negative views on both Titian and the academic
style of the Carracci were expressed frequently in

his correspondence. And although he visited
Ferrara in 1842 and took a surprisingly positive
view of Mazzolino, Garofalo, and Ortolano,
whom he described to Anne (letter 3 June 1842) as
'among the purest advocates of Christian art in
that day of declension into Paganism,' he specifi-
cally excluded Dosso Dossi. However, his view of
Dosso may have been compromised by his failure
to identify correctly the artist's autograph work;
thus he writes that 'his frescoes on the ceilings of
the old Ducal palace are amongst the most
horrible, disgusting exhibitions that the followers of M. Angelo ever bedaubed walls with',
although these are no longer considered to be by
Dosso.

Fig.40 · Titian (active 1511–died 1576)
The Triumph of Bacchus and Ariadne
National Gallery, London

1. For Titian's original, see C. Gould, *National Gallery
Catalogues: Sixteenth Century Italian Schools*, London, 1975,
pp.268–74.

2. Waagen, 1854, III, p.200.

3. For this commission, see C. Robertson, 'The Carracci
and Others in the Camera del Poggiolo at Ferrara', in
Burlington Magazine, CXXXIV, 1992, pp.417–27.
Agostino's brother Annibale had certainly seen the
Ferrara Bacchanals prior to his move to Rome in 1595
(see G. Perini, *Gli scritti dei Carracci*, Bologna, 1990, p.161).

4. The attribution of the painting to Dosso has been
endorsed by Professor Peter Humfrey. For a recent
discussion of the decoration of the Camerino and
Dosso's contribution, see A. Bayer, 'Dosso's Public: The
Este Court at Ferrara' in *Ferrara*, 1998, pp.31–40.

5. See, most recently, *Ferrara*, 1998, pp.175–8, cat.no.28.

34

ATTRIBUTED TO
JACOPO TINTORETTO
1518–1594

The Body of St Mark Removed from the Funeral Pyre

Oil on canvas, 47.5 × 47 cm

PROVENANCE: Incontri collection, Venice; whence acquired by William Spence; from whom bought by Lord Lindsay in 1856, as by Tintoretto.

EXHIBITION: London, 1930, cat.no.391, as by Tintoretto.

PRIVATE COLLECTION

Fig.41 · Tintoretto (1518–1594)
The Body of St Mark Removed from the Funeral Pyre
Galleria dell' Accademia, Venice

1. C. Ridolfi, *Le maraviglie dell'arte* (Venice, 1648), edited by D. von Hadeln, Berlin, 1914–24, II, pp.22–3.

2. P. Humfrey, *Painting in Renaissance Venice*, New Haven and London, 1995, p.226.

3. Berenson, 1957, I, p.69, accepted the Lindsay picture as an autograph work by Tintoretto.

4. P. de Vecchi, *L'opera completa del Tintoretto*, Milan, 1970, p.134, cat. no. C.18; R. Pallucchini and P. Rossi, *Tintoretto: Le opere sacre e profane*, 2 vols., Milan, 1982, I, p.239, cat.no. A.6.

5. See A. Mayer, *Tintoretto*, Munich, 1923, II, pl.66; H. Tietze, 'Bozzetti di Jacopo Tintoretto' in *Arte Veneta*, V, 1951, pp.55 ff.; Berenson, 1957, II, pl.1295; P. de Vecchi, *L'opera completa del Tintoretto*, Milan, 1970, p.105, cat.no.162a; R. Pallucchini and P. Rossi, *Tintoretto: Le opere sacre e profane*, 2 vols, Milan, 1982, I, pp.154–5, cat.no.126.

6. Letter to Anne Lindsay dated Verona, 19 June 1842.

7. H. Shapiro, *Ruskin in Italy – Letters to his Parents, 1845*, Oxford, 1972, pp.211–12 (letter of 24 September 1845).

8. N. Penny ('John Ruskin and Tintoretto' in *Apollo*, XCIX, 1974, pp.268–73) suggests that Ruskin's admiration for Tintoretto was based on the artist's adherence to Ruskinian 'Truth to Nature'.

St Mark the Evangelist (died 68 AD) preached the gospel in Egypt and founded the church in Alexandria where he became bishop. He was reviled as a magician on account of his miracles and dragged by the heathen populace across stony ground until he died. He was buried by the Christians of Alexandria and his tomb there was regarded with great reverence. In about 85 AD some Venetian traders stole the body and transported it to Venice under cover of a violent nocturnal storm. The church of San Marco was built over his remains, he was honoured as the patron saint of Venice, and his legends were frequently depicted by Venetian artists.

Since the time of Carlo Ridolfi (1648),[1] the present composition has often been described as representing the episode when St Mark's body was transported to Venice after it had been removed from the tomb in Alexandria. However, it appears rather to represent the saint's body being taken down from a funeral pyre prior to burial by his followers in Alexandria.

In 1562 Tommaso Rangone, a self-promoting Venetian physician, commissioned from Tintoretto a series of three large canvases, in which he himself figures prominently, for the Scuola Grande di San Marco in Venice: *The Body of St Mark Removed from the Funeral Pyre* and *St Mark Rescuing a Saracen from Shipwreck*, both now in the Accademia, Venice; and *The Finding of the Body of St Mark*, in the Brera, Milan.

The present sketch matches almost exactly the original design of Tintoretto's large-scale painting of this subject (fig.41). Whereas the picture in Venice has been cut down on the left hand side, the sketch shows the entire composition, including the large standing figure on the extreme left that is now missing from the final painting (it survives in mutilated form on a separate strip). The architectural background is suggestive of the Piazza San Marco in Venice, an allusion to the saint's final resting place. This sketch shares on a small scale the dramatic qualities of the final painting: 'the rapidly receding vista, the inexplicable disjunction of scale, the oppressively dark sky, and the strange, wraith-like figures of the Muslims fleeing from the storm into the arcade on the left, all contribute to a mood of eeriness and disquiet that is certainly appropriate to the miraculous nature of the event, but which is likely to have left many of Tintoretto's contemporaries uncomfortably disconcerted'.[2]

Tintoretto rarely painted preparatory oil sketches (*modelli* or *bozzetti*) and they did not form an integral part of his working practice.

However, it is by no means inconceivable that such a model was required for approval by Rangone, or by the Scuola Grande di San Marco, prior to such a major undertaking.[3]

An alternative view is to regard Lindsay's sketch as a *ricordo* or informal copy, perhaps made in Tintoretto's studio or else by a talented artist of the next generation, such as Palma Giovane. Although the traditional attribution to Tintoretto has been questioned by some specialists, it would be unwise to endorse this view too hastily, and the present exhibition offers a rare opportunity to reconsider the stylistic evidence and the status of this lively sketch.[4]

A further oil sketch attributed to Tintoretto, of horizontal format, in the Musée Royal des Beaux-Arts, Brussels, appears to represent an earlier idea for the same picture.[5] It differs from the final design in almost every respect, but is conceived in the same spirit as the Lindsay sketch, although it is executed in an even more summary manner. In any case, it can hardly be regarded as a variant copy. This adds considerable weight to the view that the Lindsay sketch may be a preparatory *bozzetto*.

Lindsay's acquisition of a painting attributed to Tintoretto and vividly reflecting the artist's mannerist style is at first sight surprising. His response to Tintoretto during his extended tour of Italy in 1842 was unfavourable: 'There is no selection, no ideal beauty, either of form or expression, but a simply copying of vulgar nature.'[6] He does not discuss sixteenth-century artists in his *Sketches*, and there is no record elsewhere of his having changed his mind. On the other hand, the young John Ruskin's dramatic change of heart and conversion to Tintoretto in 1845 is well documented and may well match Lindsay's position by the time he bought the picture. Ruskin had informed his father (letter of 24 September): 'I never was so utterly crushed to the earth before any human intellect as I was today before Tintoret ... Tintoret doesn't seem to be able to stretch himself until you give him a canvas forty feet square – and then he lashes out like a leviathan and heaven and earth come together.'[7] It was this perception of Tintoretto's spiritual and intellectual dimension in the context of the materialist culture of Renaissance Venice that appealed to Ruskin and probably to Lindsay as well.[8]

35

ATTRIBUTED TO
FRANCESCO BASSANO THE YOUNGER
1549–1592

The Presentation of Christ in the Temple

Oil on copper, 55 × 44.5 cm
PROVENANCE: Unknown.

PRIVATE COLLECTION

There is considerable room for confusion when attempting to distinguish the individual hands of the sons of Jacopo Bassano (c.1510–1592), who all began as his studio assistants and whose work was closely modelled on their father's late style. This picture has been attributed in the past to both Leandro (1559–1662) and to Gerolamo Bassano (1566–1621).[1] However, the design is a repetition, with minor variations, of a much larger composition by Francesco Bassano the Younger (1549–1592) known in two signed versions in the Národní Galerie in Prague (fig.42) and the Musée des Beaux-Arts in Rouen.[2]

A notable feature of the design is the sense of restricted, compressed space, with the onlookers in the foreground surprisingly close to the action. In this respect it differs considerably from Jacopo Bassano's dramatically foreshortened designs on similar themes, such as the *Circumcision* of 1577 in the Museo Civico, Bassano. The present picture, with its uncertain perspective, flattened forms and intimate mood, is much closer in spirit to the tradition of pastoral genre painting in which the Bassano workshop specialised.

Fig.42 · Francesco Bassano the Younger (1549–1592)
The Presentation of Christ in the Temple
Národní Galerie, Prague

1. Berenson, 1957, I, p.21, as by Leandro; Arslan, 1960, I, p.328, as close to Gerolamo.
2. See Arslan, 1960, I, pp.221–2, fig.260.

36

LEANDRO BASSANO
1557–1622

Portrait of a Widow at her Devotions

Oil on canvas, 105 × 88.5 cm

PROVENANCE: Unknown.

EXHIBITIONS: London, Burlington Fine Arts Club, *A Collection of Pictures, Furniture, Maiolica and other Object of Art*, 1934–5, cat.no.72; Manchester, City Art Gallery, *Between Renaissance and Baroque*, 1965, cat.no.24.

PRIVATE COLLECTION

The portrait shows an elderly woman dressed in widow's weeds and holding a string of rosary beads, with her wedding ring clearly displayed. She kneels at a prie-dieu, on which rests a devotional book. Above, there is a framed picture of the *Birth of the Virgin* in a style similar to that of the portrait. It presumably represents one of Leandro's own works, possibly a painting on copper similar to that attributed to his brother Francesco (cat.no.35). The portrait is an interesting document of how devotional paintings of this kind were displayed and used in a domestic setting.

The portrait is traditionally attributed to Leandro Bassano who, after training in the studio of his father Jacopo, established his own workshop in Venice in 1588.[1] He specialised in portraiture and about seventy such works are known. However, he continued to paint religious pictures in a naturalistic style, consistent with the *Birth of the Virgin* composition visible in this painting. Towards the end of his career he completed a cycle of paintings for the church of San Cassiano, Venice, including another nativity scene, the *Birth of St John the Baptist*.

There is no firm evidence that Lindsay bought either this picture or the previous one, but there is a prima facie case for supposing that it was acquired either by him, his wife or his cousins James and Anne Lindsay. Lindsay's views on Jacopo Bassano and his school are recorded in his letter to Anne of 19 June 1842:

'Tintoretto again I do not admire ... he is the vulgarest of the school except Bassano, with whom indeed he has some strong sympathies. Even Bassano however sometimes rises above himself; I went round by his native town in order to see his chef d'oeuvres, the celebrated Nativity and the Baptism of S. Lucilla; the former is really a very pretty picture, the Virgin as little of a mere portrait as could be well expected – very sweet and mild if nothing more. Bassano is a very pretty place ... the adoration of his memory there quite ridiculous – they consider him superior to Raphael; he has his first manner, his second and his third etc.'

1. Berenson, 1957, I, p.21, II, pl.1229; Arslan, 1960, I, p.257, datable *c*.1590.

37

BRITISH SCHOOL
c.1840

Portrait of Lord Lindsay

Panel, 50.2 × 37 cm

PRIVATE COLLECTION

The nineteenth-century portrait bust on the table may well be the portrait of Anne Lindsay on which her friend, the sculptor Félicie de Fauveau, was working in Florence in March 1840. It was later forwarded to Lord Lindsay and installed at Haigh Hall by the autumn of 1842, following his extended tour of Italy in that year.[1] This sympathetic portrait of Lindsay with his muse was probably painted shortly afterwards. Curiously, no record of this commission has yet come to light in the family archives or catalogues.

1. Barker, 1978, p.115; the present portrait illustrated opposite p.108. However, Barker dates this portrait c.1834, which seems too early by comparison with the portrait miniature of Lindsay dated 1829 (see fig.1 in this catalogue), and is certainly so if the bust is here correctly identified.

38

CENTRAL ITALIAN
(UMBRIA OR TUSCANY)
c.1300–1350

The Madonna Enthroned

Wood (poplar), originally covered with gesso and
painted. There are traces of blue paint on the mantle,
and pink on the face. The head and body were carved
from a single block of wood, with the back hollowed
out; the arms were carved separately and fixed with
pegs.

100 cm high, the base 28 × 23.5 cm

DESCRIPTION: The Virgin Mary, in majesty, crowned,
is seated frontally wearing a long tunic with cloak that
falls in a cowl around her upper torso and then is
gathered around her knees. Her left arm survives but
the right is missing, as is, presumably, a figure of the
Christ Child.

PRIVATE COLLECTION

This stiff, hieratic image, with its strictly frontal
Byzantine pose and swirling symmetrical draperies, is especially close to a wooden *Madonna* in the
Bayerisches Nationalmuseum in Munich,[1] and
there are others of much the same type in the
Museo Nazionale del Bargello, Florence,[2] the
church of Sant'Antonio in Montalcino,[3] and in
the Thyssen-Bornemisza Collection.[4] Carved
Madonnas of this type find their painted equiva-
lents in the works of Tuscan artists of the late
thirteenth century, such as the St Francis Master
and the Magdalene Master.[5] There are also many
points of similarity with the painted low relief
Virgin and Child attributed to Coppo di
Marcovaldo in Santa Maria Maggiore, Florence,
which probably dates from the late 1260s.[6]

1. See E. Carli, *La Scultura lignea italiana dal XII al XVI secolo*,
    Milan, 1990, pp.23–4, pl.XIX.

2. J. Lorenzelli, P. Lorenzelli and A. Veca, *Custode
    dell'imagine: Scultura Lignea Europea XII–XV secolo*, Galleria
    Lorenzelli, Bergamo, 1987, p.158, fig.18.

3. Siena, Pinacoteca Nazionale, *Scultura Dipinta: Maestri di
    legname e pittori a Siena 1250–1450*, exhibition catalogue
    edited by A. Bagnoli, 1987, pp.16–18, cat.no.1.

4. P. Williamson, *Medieval Sculpture and Works of Art: The
    Thyssen-Bornemisza Collection*, London, 1987, pp.84–7,
    cat.no.14.

5. A. Smart, *The Dawn of Italian Painting, 1250–1400*, London,
    1978, pp.8, 10, 14 and 18, figs.2, 4, 8 and 9.

6. J. White, *Art and Architecture in Italy: 1250–1400*, London,
    1966, p.111, pl.47a.

39

WORKSHOP OF MICHELE DINI,
CALLED MICHELE DA FIRENZE
active 1404–after 1443

The Virgin and Child

Terracotta, with traces of the original blue, red and
black polychromy, 66 cm high

Incised on the back: I Q

DESCRIPTION: The Virgin stands facing half right,
supporting the Christ Child with her left arm while
steadying his left foot with her right hand. She wears
thonged sandals, a shift gathered with a tie beneath her
breasts, and a mantle with kerchief over her head. The
statuette has a shallow rectangular base, with the front
corners chamfered.

PRIVATE COLLECTION

On the basis of the inscription, this terracotta
was formerly ascribed to Jacopo della Quercia
(c.1374–1438), whose style it in fact only superfi-
cially resembles. To judge from the exaggeratedly
large head and hands, the figure was originally
intended to be seen from below. The figure as a
whole is late Gothic in style, but the facial features and antique treatment of the hair suggest
some knowledge of the world of Masaccio and,
especially, of Nanni di Bartolo. It in fact shares
many of the characteristics of the work of
Michele da Firenze, who was responsible for
three major complexes in terracotta: the *Tomb of
Francesco Rosselli* in San Francesco, Arezzo (1431);
the Pellegrini Chapel in Sant'Anastasia, Verona
(1436); and an altar in the Duomo at Modena
(1442).[1] The Lindsay *Virgin and Child* is very close
in treatment to the sculptor's terracotta relief of
*The Virgin and Child with Sts John the Baptist and
James* in the Victoria and Albert Museum,[2] and to
statuettes of the *Virgin and Child* in the Bargello,
Florence,[3] and of *St Leonard* in a private collection.[4]

1. The attribution of this terracotta to Michele da Firenze
   was first proposed by Professor Martin Kemp in a letter
   to the owner dated 2 June 1994.

2. See Pope-Hennessy, 1964, I, pp.65–6, cat.no.56; III,
   pl.68.

3. Inv.no.410, described as Florentine School, fifteenth
   century.

4. See Verona, Museo di Castelvecchio, *Pisanello*, exhibition
   catalogue edited by P. Marini, 1996, cat.no.101, pp.418–19.

40

ANDREA DELLA ROBBIA
1435–1525

Lunette with the Virgin Mary Adoring the Christ Child, enclosed by an Arc of Eight Seraphim

Maiolica, the figures enamelled in white on a blue ground, the haloes gilded, the manger of the Christ Child in grey and green enamel, 69.2 × 136 cm

DESCRIPTION: The image shows the Blessed Virgin Mary adoring the Christ Child, who places his index finger on his lips. This is a clear reference to the Incarnation, to Christ as 'the word made flesh', as described in the prologue to the fourth gospel.

PROVENANCE: Lombardi-Baldi collection, Florence.

PRIVATE COLLECTION

This lunette was formerly thought to be by Luca della Robbia (1399/1400–1482), but on stylistic grounds it can be reliably attributed to his nephew Andrea. He was Luca's most talented pupil, who inherited the family house and studio in Via Guelfa, Florence, in 1485. Luca modelled only one relief of this subject, which is now in the parish church of Nynehead, Somerset, and little resembles the Lindsay lunette.[1] However, very similar figures of the kneeling Virgin Mary occur frequently in reliefs produced in Andrea della Robbia's workshop, albeit few with such carefully observed and magisterially executed drapery.[2] Such sophistication reminds one of the celebrated drapery studies on linen attributed to Leonardo da Vinci, and more particularly of the morphology of Davide Ghirlandaio's drapery. The generously gathered cloth falling in ample triangular folds, bunching to express the heels beneath, and then cascading into a fan of tucks as they fall to the floor, recurs in several images by Ghirlandaio, most notably in the *Visitation with St Mary of James and Mary Salome* commissioned by Lorenzo Tornabuoni for the church of Santa Maria Maddalena de' Pazzi (formerly the church of the Cestello), an altarpiece that was certainly known to Giovanni della Robbia.[3] It is worth considering whether the paintings of Davide Ghirlandaio simply influenced Andrea, or whether, as seems quite possible, Ghirlandaio may have provided the sculptor with a design.

It has been suggested that this lunette may be identical with the lost 'Natività di terra cotta invetriata', supplied for the renovated portal of the Arte dei Giudici e Notai in Via del Proconsolo, Florence, which was erected and paid for in November 1489.[4]

However, the Lindsay lunette is said to have come from the above mentioned monastery of Santa Maria Maddalena de' Pazzi,[5] which was founded in the fourteenth century, but was largely rebuilt between 1480 and 1492 under the direction of Giuliano da Sangallo. It still boasts a fine fresco by Perugino (1493–6) in the chapter house. If the lunette can be confirmed to have come from this church, it is most likely dates from the late 1480s or early 1490s, when extensive building and embellishing work was being undertaken. The modelling style, with an arc of seraphim, recurs in Andrea della Robbia's lunette of *The Annunciation* in the Spedale degli Innocenti in Florence, made for the Cappella Del Pugliese to surmount *The Coronation of the Virgin* painted by Piero di Cosimo in 1493.[6]

1. J. Pope-Hennessy, *Luca della Robbia*, Oxford, 1980, cat.no.50, pl.123.

2. See, for example, Fiesole, 1998, pp.122, 124, 137, 174; and especially the *Adoration of the Christ Child with God the Father and Angels* in the Cappella Brizi of the Chiesa Maggiore at La Verna (Gentilini, 1993, I, p.193). The meaning of the Christ Child's gesture in the latter is made explicit in the original inscription on the maiolica frame: VERBUM CARO FATTV. EST. DE VIRGINE. MA.

3. A. de Marchi, 'Ancora che l'arte fusse diversa' in Fiesole, 1998, pp.17–30, especially pp.22–3 (detail reproduced). The altarpiece, now in the Louvre, is reproduced in Berenson, 1963, II, fig.976.

4. Gentilini, 1993, I, pp.214–15. The document cited was published by A. Marquand, *Andrea della Robbia and his Atelier*, 1922, I, pp.93–4, n.64.

5. According to a 1913 valuation of the collection, which there is no reason to doubt.

6. Fiesole, 1998, p.178.

41

ATTRIBUTED TO
THE MASTER OF THE DAVID AND
ST JOHN STATUETTES
active late fifteenth and early sixteenth century

David Victorious

Marble, 53 cm high

DESCRIPTION: The young David stands, facing to the front, with his weight on his right leg and a cloak over his right shoulder. He wears thonged sandals and places his left arm on his hip, holding a sling shot, and in his right hand he holds a sword broken off at the hilt. There are two holes bored in the rocky base, presumably for attaching the head of Goliath (missing).

PRIVATE COLLECTION

The boy David took up the challenge to single combat with Goliath, the giant leader of the Philistines. By killing Goliath with a stone from his sling, he became leader and eventually king of the Israelites (Samuel 1). This marble statuette is clearly related to a distinctive group of terracotta figures of David and St John the Baptist, four of which are in the Victoria and Albert Museum.[1] These figures are emphatically Florentine in iconography and style – for the Florentines venerated the Baptist as the patron of their city and, as Republicans, they greatly admired and identified with the hero David. Iconographically, there is a dependence on Verrocchio's bronze David in the Bargello, Florence, datable to before 1469, and on Michelangelo's marble David now in the Accademia, which was completed in 1504.[2] The sculptor responsible for this group of statuettes has not been identified. The names of the young Jacopo Sansovino and Leonardo del Tasso have been proposed, but he seems rather to have been a sculptor of no great originality close to Benedetto da Maiano.[3]

1. Pope-Hennessy, 1964, I, pp.191-4, cat.nos.169-71; III, pls.180-3. Further relevant examples of this master's work are in the former Kaiser Friedrich Museum, Berlin (acc.no.5011/Sch. 227) and the National Gallery of Art, Washington (Samuel H. Kress Collection, acc.no.1943-4-81).

2. For both the Verrocchio and the Michelangelo, see D. Karl, Il David del Verrocchio, Museo Nazionale del Bargello, Florence, 1987.

3. This group of figures has also in the past been ascribed to Andrea Sansovino, Baccio da Montelupo, and even to the Sienese sculptors Francesco di Giorgio and Giacomo Cozzarelli, but the connection seems more generic than specific. Benedetto da Maiano's late marble St Sebastian of c.1497, in the Oratory of the Misericordia, Florence, offers many stylistic points of similarity (see J. Poeschke, Donatello and his World, New York, 1993, p.476, pl.292). For a closely related terracotta in the collection of the late Arthur M. Sackler, see Washington, National Gallery of Art, New York, Metropolitan Museum of Art and Harvard University, Fogg Art Museum, Finger Prints of the Artist: European Terracotta Sculpture from the Arthur M. Sackler Collections, exhibition catalogue by C. Avery, 1980-2, pp.44-5, cat.no.8.

42

ATTRIBUTED TO
ALESSANDRO VITTORIA
1525-1608

St John the Baptist

Marble, 82.5 cm high

DESCRIPTION: The saint, bearded with long curling hair, clad in a goat-skin tied around his waist and attached over his shoulders with leather thongs, strides forward, a small cup clasped to his chest in his right hand; his left hand is curved to clasp a cross (now missing), and a lamb sits at his feet.

PRIVATE COLLECTION

The itinerant preacher-saint is shown conventionally clad as he was in the desert, with the cup that he used for baptising Christ in the River Jordan and the Lamb of God at his feet, a reference to his dictum 'Ecce Agnus Dei' ('Behold the Lamb of God [that takes away the sins of the world]', from John 1:29–36). St John was beheaded by Herod Antipas at the behest of Herodias's daughter, Salome (Matthew 14:112).

Figures of St John of this type and scale are commonly found standing as the finial of a baptismal font or at the centre of an *acquasantiera* (holy water stoup). The pose, with its marked *contrapposto* (a serpentine configuration with the legs facing in one direction, the torso another, and the head following the same direction as the legs), is reminiscent of several sculptures by Jacopo Sansovino (1486–1570), the great Florentine sculptor and architect who worked for much of his career in Venice.[1] This sculpture has indeed traditionally been attributed to Sansovino, but the style seems closer to that of his most brilliant pupil, Alessandro Vittoria. It is particularly like in carving and facture to Vittoria's figure of *St John the Baptist*, which still stands on the *acquasantiera* to the right of the entrance in San Zaccaria, Venice, and for which he was paid two ducats on 26 April 1550.[2]

It is instructive to compare this marble with Jacopo Sansovino's signed *St John the Baptist* of 1534-7, now in the Cornaro Chapel in the church of the Frari, Venice.[3] The latter figure's effortlessly relaxed pose, high polish, and lovingly described naturalistic details - so thoroughly Tuscan and harking back to the *Quattrocento* - is a world away from the present robust, athletic St John, where the rendering of musculature and demonstration of anatomy shows a particular interest in Michelangelo. These characteristics suggest that this could be a relatively early work, of astonishing quality, by Vittoria. With much of the vigour of his marble *St Jerome* of c.1564, on the Zane altar in the Frari, this small marble anticipates in reverse the pose of some of his later bronze statuettes, such as the *Jupiter* of c.1580 in the Kunsthistorisches Museum, Vienna.[4]

Although there is no record of when and where Lord Lindsay acquired this statue, we can be fairly sure that it was indeed he who bought it, for it is clearly distinguishable in a photograph of the drawing room of his house at Dunecht (see fig.6).

1. For Sansovino, see Boucher, 1991.

2. See Trento, 1999, pp.16–19.

3. Boucher, 1991, II, cat.no.13, pl.v and figs.93–5; Trento, 1999, pp.214–17, cat.no.12.

4. Trento, 1999, p.129, fig.4; pp.352–3, cat.no.78; Boucher, 1991, II, figs.451–2.

43

SCHOOL OF BURGUNDY
(POSSIBLY FROM THE WORKSHOP OF
ÉTIENNE BOBILLET AND PAUL
MOSSELMAN)
*c.*1450

Two Monks in Mourning ('Pleurants')

[A] A cowled monk, the right side of his bearded face revealed by the hood drawn back, his hands now missing.

Carved inscription on the hood: [? jehan clerc]

Alabaster, 39.5 cm high

[B] A cowled monk, facing front, his face hidden by a voluminous hood, hands folded in front holding the Office of the Dead.

Alabaster, flecked with purple veining on the reverse; traces of green paint on the base, 39.5 cm high

PRIVATE COLLECTION

NOTE: Having been selected for the exhibition, it subsequently emerged that these two figures were not owned by Lord Lindsay himself, but were bought by his grandson from Durlacher Brothers, the London dealers, in February 1920.

1. The literature on the tomb and its sculptures is extensive. See A. Lecoy de la Marche, *Extraits des comtes du roi René*, Paris, 1873, pp.56–7; A. de Champeaux and P. Gauchery, *Les travaux d'art exécutés par Jean de France, duc de Berry*, Paris, 1894; P. Gauchery, 'Le Palais du duc Jean et la Sainte-Chapelle de Bourges ...', in *Mémoires de la Société des Antiquaires du Centre*, 1919–20, pp.37–77; idem, 'Renseignements complémentaires sur la vie et les travaux de Jean de France, duc de Berry, d'après des documents nouveaux' in *Mémoires de la Société des Antiquaires du Centre*, 1921, pp.195–211; G. Tröscher, *Die Burgundische Plastik des Ausgehenden Mittelalters und ihre Wirkungen aus die europäische Kunst*, Frankfurt, 1940, pp.74–8; P. Pradel, 'Nouveaux documents sur le tombeau de Jean de Berry, Frère de Charles V', in *Foundation Eugène Piot, Monuments et Mémoires*, I,1, 1957, pp.141–57; B. Bessard, 'Three Berry Mourners' in *The Metropolitan Museum Journal*, 1968, pp.171–6; M. Beaulieu, in exhibition catalogue, *Les Pleurants dans l'art du moyen-âge en Europe*, Musée des Beaux Arts de Dijon, Palais des ducs du Bourgogne, 1971, pp.36–7, cat.nos.66–90; M. Meiss, with the assistance of S.O. Dunlop Smith and E.H. Beatson, *French Painting in the Time of Jean de Berry: The Limbourgs and their Contemporaries*, New York and London, 1974.

These two mourners were carved for the tomb of Jean de France, Duke of Berry, Duke of the Auvergne, Count of Poitou, etc. (1340–1416), at Bourges.[1] The son of King Jean le Bon of France, and brother of King Charles V of France, the Duc de Berry was undoubtedly the most distinguished patron of art in northern Europe at that time. He was responsible for commissioning some three hundred illuminated manuscripts, about a hundred of which still survive; he was the patron of the great sculptor, Claus Sluter, and of the Limbourg Brothers; he collected coins and medals avidly; and he owned pseudo-ancient cameos (now in the Louvre), a cycle of tapestries (now in the Cloisters Museum, New York), and a great enamelled gold reliquary (now in the British Museum). He commissioned his tomb in 1405 from Jean de Cambrai, the collaborator of André Beauneveu, to be erected in the Sainte-Chapelle of Bourges, constructed next to the Ducal Palace. The tomb followed the traditional format, with the decaying figure of the duke below, glimpsed through an arcade, with a black marble slab above on which lay an effigy of the deceased in all his finery, as if asleep, and around the four sides, within the arcading, on alternating circular and triangular pedestals, the figures of forty monks, heavily cowled as if performing the rites of the Office of the Dead for the departed soul of the duke.

The original tomb was removed in 1756 from the Sainte-Chapelle to the crypt of the cathedral at Bourges. During the French Revolution, the tomb was vandalised: much of the structure was used for hard-core and, in 1793, the crypt was adapted for use as an arsenal. Many of the sculptures were saved, however. Ten of the mourners remain at Bourges, two are in the Metropolitan Museum of Art in New York, two more are in the Hermitage in St Petersburg, one is in the Institut Néerlandais in Paris, one (lacking its head) in the Musée Rodin, and eight others are recorded in private collections. The present pair is apparently unpublished. A reconstruction of the original tomb in plaster was made by the architect Paul Gauchery, and is still at Bourges.

The tomb formed part of a distinctive series, all incorporating mourners, like those of Philip the Bold and John the Fearless, both Dukes of Burgundy, which are now in the Museum at Dijon, and of Charles I de Bourbon at Souvigny, from which all the mourners are now missing.

The Duc de Berry tomb, although begun in 1405, was unfinished at the duke's death in 1416. It was still incomplete in 1450, so the late duke's great-nephew, King Charles VII, commissioned Étienne Bobillet and Paul Mosselman to complete the series of mourners. These mourners, in ample habits, resemble closely the celebrated figures carved by Claus Sluter and Claus de Werve from 1381 onwards for the tomb of Duke Philip the Bold in the Charterhouse of Champol.

The inscription on one of the present pair of mourners, evidently a signature, is incised into the back of the hood and appears to read '[Je]han Clerc' (fig.43). This sculptor, presumably an unrecorded collaborator of Bobillet and Mosselman, may have been related to either Jehan le Clereq, a painter living in Tournai who died in 1500, or to Jean de Clerc, a painter working in Bruges at the end of the fifteenth century, or even to Barthélemy Clerc, the miniaturist working in 1447 for King René.

Fig.43 · Detail of cat.43 showing the signature incised into the sculpture

44

FRENCH SCHOOL
(CHAMPAGNE, POSSIBLY TROYES)
c.1530

Fortified Tower

Limestone, 80.6 cm high; base: 23 × 20 cm

DESCRIPTION: A flamboyant gothic tower, octagonal in section, divided into four storeys, including a simple base. The taller, lower section, like smooth ashlar, with a richly moulded string course, is pierced on one face by a door (complete with wrought-iron strap hinges and box lock) reached by a curved stair, with an ogival crocketted canopy above enclosing a small figure; the second, squatter storey, above a less emphatic string course, is circular in section, pierced by domestic windows with flattened ogival heads, projecting moulded window ledges and cross transoms. The crowning storey has machicolations, four corner bartizans, and a rose window with gothic tracery. There is a hole drilled in the top for attachment.

PRIVATE COLLECTION

The tower was almost certainly carved originally as an attribute of a statue of St Barbara, but has become detached from the figure. According to *The Golden Legend*, Barbara was a virgin of great beauty whose father, Dioscorus, shut her up in a tower to discourage her many suitors. Discovering that she had become a Christian, Dioscorus resolved to kill her. He denounced her to the authorities, who tortured her, but she refused to renounce the faith, whereupon her father was ordered to put her to death. This done, he was immediately struck by lightning and reduced to ashes. This spurious legend dates back to the seventh century. Because of her father's fate, St Barbara was invoked against lightning, and she became the patron saint of gunners and miners.

The architecture of the tower, which shows no reference to the Italian Renaissance, is fundamentally Flemish or Burgundian, and later in date than one might imagine. It is strongly reminiscent of Hector Sohier's work on the east end of the church of St Pierre in Caen, datable to c.1528-45, and to some of the Troyen sculptural details of the time.[1] An oak figure of *St Barbara* attributed to Jean le Pot at the Musée Departemental de l'Oise at Beauvais gives a good idea of how St Barbara would have looked beside her attribute.[2]

1. A. Blunt, *Art and Architecture in France, 1500–1700*, London, 1953, pp.7, 17, pl.4; C. Avery, 'Sculpture from Troyes in the Victoria and Albert Museum' in *Studies in European Sculpture II*, London, 1988, pp.103–35, especially p.114, fig.18 and p.122. See also R. Koechlin and J. Marquet de Vasselot, *La Sculpture à Troyes et dans la Champagne Méridionale au XVIe Siècle*, Paris, 1900.

2. J.-L. Champion (ed.), *Mille Sculpteurs des Musées de France*, Paris, 1998, pp.180–1, fig.370.

45

MAIOLICA, DERUTA OR FAENZA
c.1520–30

Dry-drug Jar ('albarello')

28 cm high

DESCRIPTION: With slightly concave sides, the foot and rim decorated with concentric bands of yellow and blue, with a narrow frieze of short blue stripes at the top and bottom. Painted in a palette of dark blue, green, ochre, and manganese. On a white ground across the front, within a generously furled banderole, there appears the Gothic black-letter inscription: *capelletti*

PRIVATE COLLECTION

It is difficult to place where this handsome and distinctive jar was made. Stylistically, it resembles an albarello in the Victoria and Albert Museum, of unidentified origin,[1] and another at Limoges, where it is described as Castel Durante.[2] Of superior design and quality to either of these pieces, the Lindsay albarello was probably made in Faenza, although Deruta should not be ruled out. The inscription 'capelletti' is a reference to the herb *Capillus Veneris* (True Maidenhair) or *Adiantum capillus Veneris* (Venus Hair), the dried fronds of which were used medicinally.[3]

1. Rackham, 1977, cat.no.541, pl.84.

2. Giacomotti, 1974, pp.240–41, cat.no.789.

3. R.E.A. Drey, *Apothecary Jars*, London, 1978, p.192.

46

MAIOLICA, FAENZA
*c.*1490

Jug ('boccale')

32 cm high

DESCRIPTION: Of generous form, with pinched spout and broad strap handle, painted in a palette of manganese, ochre, green, and blue, with, in the centre below the lip, a shield of arms consisting of confronted herons drinking from a chalice, the shield within a circular reserve decorated with concentric bands of scale ornament and peacock feathers, the remainder of the body decorated all over with so-called 'bryony-flowers'.

PRIVATE COLLECTION

A large jug of considerable beauty and rarity, its form and decoration derive in part from the Valencian ('Hispano-Moresque') lustreware then being imported into Italy in large quantities. The Italian potters at that time could not produce their own lustre, and so they concentrated instead on elaborate polychrome decoration. Jugs such as this mark the shift in Italian pottery production from the purely utilitarian to the consciously artistic.[1] Several Florentine jugs very similar to the exhibited one have been published, and a closely comparable example appears in Carlo Crivelli's *Immaculate Conception* in the National Gallery, London, which is signed and dated 1492. The style and decoration of the Lindsay jug is, however, more closely related to Faenza, and is very similar to two jugs ascribed to Faenza in the Victoria and Albert Museum.[2]

The arms on the present jug may have been intended to refer loosely to those of the Camaldolese Monastery outside Florence, founded by St Romuald in 1012. Similar arms recur on the Andrea della Robbia workshop altarpiece with the *Madonna and Saints* in the Chapel of St Anthony in the Chiesa Maggiore, Camaldoli, but there the birds are shown as doves *argent* (white) flanking the chalice rather than herons *purpure* (purple).[3] These arms recur on another large Faenza jug by Virgiliotto Calamelli, dating from the mid-sixteenth century, now in the Museo Nazionale del Bargello, Florence.[4]

1. For a detailed discussion of Florentine jugs of this type, see G. Cora, *Storia della Maiolica di Firenze e del Contado, Secoli XIV e XV*, Florence, 1973, II, pls.168 c, 260 b, and 335, fig.10, where they are classified as 'type VII b'.

2. Rackham, 1977, p.32, cat. nos 115–16. See also Giacomotti, 1974, pp.22–41, where this class of pottery is described as 'Florence ou Faenza'.

3. See A. Marquand, *Andrea della Robbia and his Atelier*, Princeton, 1972 (reprint of the 1922 edition), II, pp.133–6, cat.no.262.

4. Inv.no.1961; gift of the Amici del Bargello, 1991.

47

MAIOLICA (LUSTREWARE), DERUTA
c.1510–40

Lustreware 'Bella Donna' Dish

53.5 cm diameter; broken and repaired

DESCRIPTION: Painted with a half-length portrait of a beautiful woman, her hair partly gathered in a snood, in profile to left, in blue and yellowish-golden lustre. The border, in the same palette, decorated '*a quartieri*' with alternate lozenges, panels of fish-scaling, and stylised foliage. The inscription on the banderole to the left of the sitter, in abbreviated dialect, appears to read: NON E SI VAC[U]O FIO E CHE. NO. I BIA[N]CA O CASCA (It is not so vain [to try], for the penalty of inaction is failure).

PRIVATE COLLECTION

So-called 'Bella Donna' dishes of this type are notoriously difficult to date with much precision. They were very popular, and the designs were presumably taken from reversible pricked-paper cartoons, reflecting the modish influence of Umbrian artists. Perugian artists like Giovanni Battista Caporali (documented 1497–1555) and Domenico Alfani (c.1480–after 1559), late followers of Perugino both of whom painted altarpieces for Deruta, may conceivably have been responsible for supplying the original cartoons for maiolica dishes of this kind.[1]

Two closely related examples of this dish exist in the Louvre, but with the sitter facing in the opposite direction, in profile to right;[2] others, with the sitter in the same direction, are in the Nelson-Atkins Museum of Art, Kansas City, and the Victoria and Albert Museum.[3]

1. See, for example, F. Todini, *La Pittura Umbra*, Milan 1989, I, pp.18–20, 54–5; II, figs.1453, 1455, 1456–7, 1463, and 1467.

2. Giacomotti, 1974, pp.178–80, cat.nos.584–5.

3. Rackham, 1977, I, p.159, cat.no.480; II, pl.75.

48

MAIOLICA (LUSTREWARE), DERUTA
c.1530–50

Lustreware Dish with St Francis Receiving the Stigmata

41 cm diameter; broken and repaired

DESCRIPTION: Painted in blue and yellowish-golden lustre, with a kneeling figure of St Francis receiving the Stigmata (the wounds of Christ), from a figure of Christ on the Cross, supported by a winged seraph. The saint kneels amongst luxuriant foliage, and is warmed by the sun's rays. The border, in the same palette, is decorated with formalised scrolling foliage.

PRIVATE COLLECTION

The maiolica painter has probably added the flowers and the sun (references to *The Little Flowers of St Francis* and the *Canticle of the Sun* respectively) to the original sophisticated cartoon, which was perhaps supplied by, or derived from, a good contemporary Umbrian artist. The chapel visible in the background is probably the Porzuincola, below Assisi, but in every other respect the subject is respresented as described by the Franciscan theologian St Bonaventura, the Seraphic Teacher and a Doctor of the Church. The subject of St Francis painted on maiolica was particularly popular at Deruta, for Assisi is nearby. Such lustred dishes evidently continued to be manufactured for several decades, for one similar to this, in the Ariana Museum, Geneva, has a border decorated with the arms of Pope Pius IV Medici (1559–65). Another comparable example is in the National Museums of Scotland.[1]

1. C. Curnow, *Italian Maiolica in the National Museums of Scotland*, Edinburgh, 1992, p.43, cat.no.34.

49

MAIOLICA, CASTEL DURANTE
OR URBINO
c.1525–50

'Cerquate' Dish

42 cm diameter

DESCRIPTION: With moulded emplacement for a
ewer, painted in the centre with a Stag at Lodge in blue,
green and yellow, surrounded by a fruiting laurel
wreath, the wide, shaped border painted all over with
six pairs of interlaced oak branches in yellow and black
on a turquoise ground.

PRIVATE COLLECTION

According to Cipriano Piccolpasso, in his I tre libri
dell'arte del Vasaio – a manuscript treatise now in
the Victoria and Albert Museum, compiled
around 1557 but not published in his lifetime –
this type of design, with an all over oak-leaf
pattern, was called 'cerquate' by the Castel
Durante potters, explaining that 'in the shade of
[the oak] we live happily, so that this can be called
the Urbino style of painting'. The oak (quercia or
rovere in Italian) was part of the arms of the Della
Rovere family, Dukes of Urbino: azure (blue) an
oak tree eradicated (uprooted), or (gold) the four
branches proper entwined in saltire (crossed).

Other closely related dishes of the same date
are in the British Museum,[1] the Wallace Collection,[2] and, of a slightly earlier date, at the Musée
de Cluny.[3]

1. London, British Museum, Ceramic Art of the Italian
   Renaissance, exhibition catalogue by T. Wilson, 1987,
   pp.83–4, cat.no.125.

2. A.V.B. Norman, The Wallace Collection: Catalogue of Ceramics
   I: Pottery, Faience, Stoneware, London, 1976, pp.61–2,
   cat.no.C16.

3. Giacomotti, 1974, p.239, cat.no.786.

50

MAIOLICA, CASTEL DURANTE
c.1530–40

Small Dish ('tondino')

27 cm diameter

DESCRIPTION: Painted in colours, with in the centre a landscape with a youth (Patience) holding an hour-glass, seated in a chariot drawn by two snails, attempting to catch up with a hare that bounds ahead of him. The broad border is decorated with a damascened pattern in *bianco sopra bianco*, and the narrow rim is enclosed by a wreath of oak leaves and acorns in green enamel.

Marked in blue on reverse: H

Small Dish ('tondino')

26.7 cm diameter

DESCRIPTION: Painted in colours, with in the centre a landscape with a naked woman holding a cornucopia (Abundance). The border and rim are decorated as above.

Marked by the painter in blue on the reverse: H

PRIVATE COLLECTION

1. See Giacomotti, 1974, p.238, cat.no.783; D.J. Chompret, *Répertoire de la Majolique Italienne*, Milan, 1986 (reprint of the 1949 edition), I, p.20; II, p.20, figs.152–3.

2. For this dish, see J.V.G. Mallet, 'In Bottega di Maestro Guido Durantino in Urbino', in *Burlington Magazine*, CXXIX, 1987, pp.284–98, figs.8 and 8a.

3. Ibid., fig.7a

4. Rackham, 1977, I, pp.202–3, cat.no.610; II, pl.96.

This very fine pair of dishes appears to have formed part of a service (*credenza*) of small display dishes. Another dish from the same service, of similar size, with a female figure (possibly Prudence) with double profile, standing looking at herself in a hand mirror and holding in her left hand an open compass, the points resting on the trunk of a felled tree, is in the Musée Ceramique de Sèvres.[1] It too is marked on the back by the painter with the unexplained capital 'H' in blue. The style of figure drawing seems consistent with some pieces from the workshop of Guido (Fontana) Durantino at Castel Durante. This is not the place to expand the argument, but it seems possible that the 'H' might stand for Horatio (Orazio), the ablest of the three sons of Guido Durantino. Born in 1510, by the 1530s he would have been in his twenties and quite capable of such excellent painting. Were this the case, these pieces would pre-date Orazio's earliest recorded signed dish of 1542 (formerly in the Schlossmuseum, Berlin), which represents *The Contest between the Muses and the Pierides*, taken from a print by Jacopo Caraglio after Rosso Fiorentino.[2] The 'H' mark, which does not correspond with Orazio's later monogram,[3] might conceivably be a mark of ownership, but on istoriato pieces, which were costly, one would expect the owner to identify commissioned pieces with a shield of arms or crest on the front of the dish.

A closely related but much larger dish, dated 1544, is in the Victoria and Albert Museum.[4]

51

MAIOLICA, FLORENCE (MONTELUPO)
c.1609–21

Jug ('boccale')

38 cm high

DESCRIPTION: Painted in a palette of blue, yellow, ochre, brown, and green. At the centre, below the lip, is the shield of arms ('stemma') of Medici impaling Hapsburg, surmounted by a ducal coronet, the arms contained within a circular reserve which is enclosed by twin cornucopiae filled with fruiting foliage. The large strap handle terminates with a painted crescent.

PRIVATE COLLECTION

The crescent painted at the base of the handle, the position where Montelupo potters invariably marked their jugs, is presumably the emblem of a potter and not a mark of ownership. The jug represents the arms of Grand Duke Cosimo II de' Medici (1590–1621), who inherited the dukedom in 1609, and of his wife, Maria Maddalena of Austria, daughter of Archduke Charles and sister of Archduke Maximilian. The actual marriage ceremony was performed in the Jesuit church at Graz, Austria, on 14 September 1608, with Paolo Giordano Orsini, Duke of Bracciano, serving as Cosimo's proxy. Maria Maddalena did not arrive for her formal triumphal entry into Florence until 18 October; the great nuptial banquet took place the following day, and the wedding festivities continued until 5 November. This jug may have been made in association with these festive occasions, and should not date from later than 28 February 1621, when Cosimo II died.[1] However, the use of this combination of arms evidently continued, incorrectly, after Cosimo's death, for they appear on a wet-drug jar dated 1626 in the Bargello, Florence.[2]

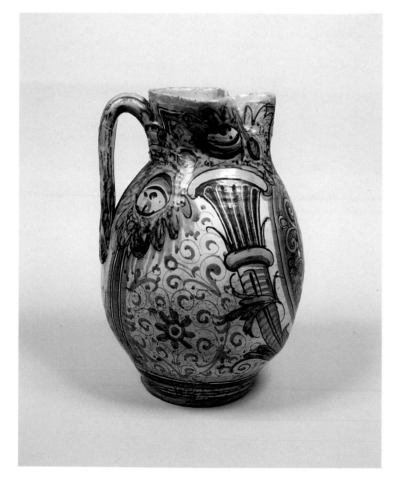

1. Florence, Uffizi, Gabinetto Disegni e Stampe, *Feste e apparati Medicei da Cosimo I a Cosimo II*, exhibition catalogue by G. Gaeta Bertelà and A. Petrioli Tofani, 1969, pp.102–5, 192–3.

2. G. Conti, *Museo Nazionale di Firenze, Palazzo del Bargello: Catalogo delle maioliche*, Florence, 1971, cat.no.621.

52

FLORENTINE SCHOOL
late fifteenth century

The Annunciation

Lampass (a figured woven textile of mixed linen and silk)

74 × 22.5 cm (sight size)

DESCRIPTION: A vertical length of figured textile of repeating design, gold on a pink ground (faded). The background is formed by the main warps and wefts, while the pattern is formed by weft floats secured to a binding warp.

PRIVATE COLLECTION

This is an attractive specimen of a textile border, probably manufactured in Florence or Prato. Such bands, called ophreys, were applied to ecclesiastical vestments such as chasubles, copes and dalmatics. Other comparable examples are in the Bargello and the Museo degli Argenti, Florence, the collection of the late Sir Harold Acton, Villa La Pietra, Florence, the Victoria and Albert Museum, and the Musée Historique des Tissus at Lyons; a further large group formerly in the Steiglitz Collection, was transferred to the Hermitage Museum, St Petersburg, in 1923. They show subjects such as the Assumption of the Virgin, the Resurrection, the Blessed Trigramma of San Bernardino adored by standing or kneeling angels, and the Virgin kneeling adoring the Christ Child. In spite of the nature of the weave being intractable for the finest work, the subjects, rather than being taken from woodcuts, were designed by such artists as Bartolomeo di Giovanni (active 1470 – died 1501(?)) and Raffaellino del Garbo (c.1466–1524). A drawing by Raffaellino of *The Angel of the Annunciation*, designed for just such a textile and pricked for transfer, belongs to Rugby School, Rugby.[1]

1. For examples of textiles of this kind, see A.C. Weibel, 'Woven Orphreys' in *Bulletin of the Detroit Institute of Arts*, XVI, 6, 1937, pp.96–9; P. Peri, *Museo Nazionale del Bargello: Bordi Figurati del Rinascimento*, Florence, 1990, pp.72–6. For the activities of even more distinguished Florentine artists as designers of embroideries, see A Garzelli, *Il ricamo nella attività artistica di Pollaiuolo, Botticelli, and Bartolommeo di Giovanni*, Florence, 1973.

53

FLEMISH SCHOOL (BRUSSELS)
c.1525–40
Possibly based on a design by Bernard van Orley (c.1488–1541) or an artist in his circle.

Tapestry (wool and silk), 96.5 × 303 cm

DESCRIPTION: To judge from its format, this tapestry was probably intended either as an antependium, to hang in front of an altar, or as a dorsal, to hang behind one. It is woven with, in the centre, the *Agony in the Garden*, flanked to the left by the *Standing Virgin and Child* and to the right by a monastic saint wearing a white habit and holding a pastoral staff and a model of a church. The church has a high-pitched roof and a *flèche* over the crossing and the saint is further identified with the woven initials 'S.B.'. He is most likely to be St Bernard, but could be St Benedict or St Bruno. The figures are set in a richly verdant, mountainous landscape, the three sections of the composition subdivided by mannerist columns consisting of clusters of four fluted pilasters, the shafts widening and breaking at a ring in the centre, supported on tall, richly moulded plinths. Attached to the columns, which support foliate brackets, are croziers from which are suspended a lozenge with the arms of the donatrix to the left (*gules, lozengy argent 3, 3, 3 and 1*) and, to the right, a shield with the arms of the donor (*sable, a shaped bend dexter, chequy argent and gules*). The landscape composition is contained within a rich border of flowers, fruit, and vegetables, inhabited by birds, with oval medallions at the corners representing the symbols of the four Evangelists.

PRIVATE COLLECTION

Christ is shown kneeling in prayer before the Host, placed on a rocky outcrop. The three sleeping apostles behind him should, according to the gospels, be Peter, James and John. However, the foremost of them, who in other respects conforms to traditional representations of Peter, has a sword, the usual attribute of St Paul, tucked under his arm, while the younger apostle at the left has no halo and is accompanied by a green parrot perched on a branch directly above. In the background, Judas Iscariot, the betrayer, leads soldiers with torches through the gate of the Garden of Gethsemane while clutching his bag of silver.

Stylistically, the tapestry dates from c.1525–40, when Brussels was a world-renowned centre for tapestry production. The subject of *The Agony in the Garden* was not uncommon among suites of Brussels tapestries representing the Passion cycle. The Lindsay tapestry, however, was conceived as a single, independent piece. With its flanking figures of the *Virgin and Child* and *St Bernard* (?), and with two shields displayed prominently, it must have been woven for a specific destination. The figure style of the principal scene is conservative, looking back to the imagery of Van der Weyden, Memlinc, and even Dürer, but the flanking figures are more modern and Italianate. The elaborate pilasters that sub-divide the composition, with their leafy brackets and strings of pearls, recall the Antwerp Mannerists' fascination

with Italian sources. The designer of the tapestry was evidently a Flemish 'Romanist' in the immediate circle of Barend van Orley (c.1488–1541), such as Pieter Coeck van Aelst (1502–1550), or Dirck Vellert (1511–1547).[1] The border, densely ornamented with a frieze of fruit and vegetables, is characteristic of the studio of Pieter de Pannemaker and recurs in the *editio princeps* of the *Hunts of Maximilian* tapestry series (c.1538; Louvre, Paris), which were designed by Van Orley.

The arms on the left of the Lindsay tapestry are those of a lady, probably an Abbess, from the noble house of Lalaing of Brabant, Counts of Hoogstraten from 1518 and Counts of Lalaing from 1522.[2] Antoine de Lalaing, Governor of Holland, and a special favourite of the Emperor Charles V, received the Order of the Golden Fleece from that monarch at Brussels in 1516.[3]

The Lalaing arms appear on a cycle of tapestries woven with the legends of St Anthony of Egypt and of St Elizabeth in the great church of St Catherine, Hoogstraten, which was built by Count Antoine and his wife, Elizabeth of Culemberg, from 1525 onwards.[4] The Lady Chapel is dated 1535. The Lalaing arms recur in the stained glass of the church designed and painted by Vellert and Van Orley.[5] Vellert's window, showing Charles de Lalaing and his wife, Margaretha van Croy-Chimay, is dated

1528. A payment to Van Orley is recorded for a painting of 'La vertue de patience', thought to be the 'Job Altarpiece' now in the Musée Royal des Beaux-Arts in Brussels and dated 1521, which was painted for the chambers of the Regent Margaret in the Château de Lalaing.[6] Further research may establish whether this tapestry was also originally destined for St Catherine's, Hoogstraten, or, alternatively, whether it was commissioned by a member of the Lalaing family for a monastic foundation within the province.

1. For Van Orley's tapestries, see A. Wauters, *Bernard van Orley*, Brussels, 1893; C. Terlinden et al., *Bernard van Orley, 1488–1541*, Brussels, 1943; G. Delmarcel, 'A propos de deux tentures de tapisseries bruxelloises d'après Bernard van Orley', in *Revue Belge d'Archéologie et d'Histoire de l'Art*, IX, 1991, pp.121–33.

2. J.B. Riestap, *Armorial Général*, Berlin, 1934, p.9.

3. Bruges, Musée Communal des Beaux-Arts, *La Toison d'Or: Cinq Siècles d'Art et d'Histoire*, exhibition catalogue, 1962, pp.38–9.

4. Photographs in the Textile Department of the Victoria and Albert Museum, London (XXVIIa, nos.4763-5- 1927).

5. For the Hoogstraten stained glass, see *Onze-Kunst*, 1922– 23, pp.104–7, figs.14–17; J. Helbig, 'Les auteurs des verrières d'Hoogstraten' in *Revue Belge d'Archéologie et d'Histoire de l'Art*, XVIII, 1949, p.102; G. Marlier, *La Renaissance flamande: Pierre Coeck d'Alost*, Brussels, 1966, pp.359–62.

6. M. Wynn Ainsworth, 'Bernard van Orley' in the *Dictionary of Art*, 1996, 23, pp.524–8.

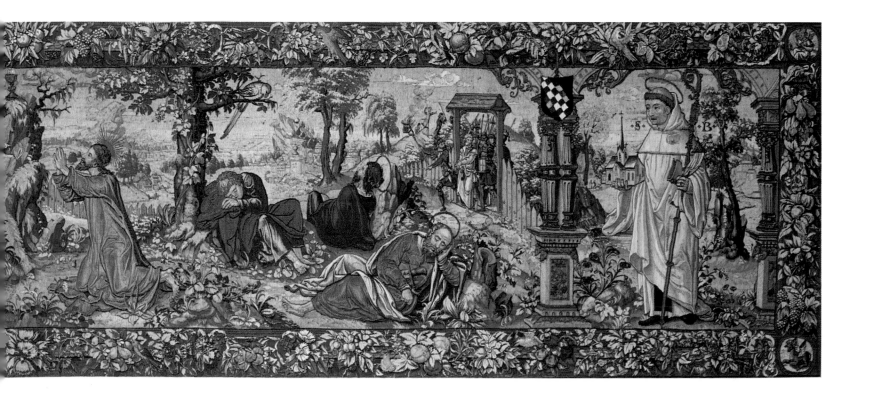

54

Homiliarius (Collection of Sermons)

Manuscript on vellum, 295 × 222mm, ff.143, 27 lines to the page.

Bought by Bernard Quaritch at the Libri sale in March 1859 for £31, and sold to Lord Lindsay the following month for £36; bound, probably for Libri, in calf over boards.

REFERENCES: James, 1921, no.12; L.W. Jones, 'Dom Victor Perrin and Three Manuscripts of Luxeuil', *Bulletin of the John Rylands Library*, XXIII (1939), pp.178–81; Barker, 1978, pp.175–6.

LENT BY THE JOHN RYLANDS UNIVERSITY LIBRARY OF MANCHESTER

Written about the year 800 in the minuscule hand peculiar to the Abbey of Luxeuil in eastern France. The homilies are by St Fulgentius, St Severianus and other early fathers. The book was still at Luxeuil in 1790, when it was listed in the catalogue of the Abbey library by Prior Vautherot; an extensive description by the archivist, Dom Victor Perrin (died 1740), is bound with the manuscript. For Lord Lindsay, this was the pick of the manuscripts he had bought at the Libri sale: 'But none of these are more pleasing (in its peculiar way) than the tattered and battered *Homilies* of the 8th century, a most interesting relic of the early church, and which will stand well at the commencement of the series of service books and liturgies in Lord L's possession'.

55

Evangelia (Gospel Book)

Manuscript on vellum, 298 × 203mm, ff.182, 27 lines to the page.

Bought by Lord Lindsay at the Libri sale in March 1859, on commission through Bernard Quaritch, for £150, and bound at the time in morocco by Francis Bedford.

REFERENCES: James, 1921, no.9. B. Bischoff, *Lorsch im Spiegel seiner Handschriften*, Munich, 1974, pp.36–7, 41, 76; Barker, 1978, pp.175–6.

LENT BY THE JOHN RYLANDS UNIVERSITY LIBRARY OF MANCHESTER

Written in the first quarter of the ninth century in a fine Carolingian minuscule script at the Benedictine abbey of Lorsch in south-west Germany, a famous centre for the production of finely written and illuminated books. The miniature of St Mark, which Lindsay characterised as 'a valuable and admirably preserved specimen of the peculiar painting of the school founded or rather reinvigorated by Charlemagne', is a direct copy of that in the famous Lorsch Gospels (now divided between the Biblioteca Documentara Batthyaneum, Alba Julia, Romania, and the Bibliotheca Apostolica in the Vatican; one cover is in the Victoria and Albert Museum, the other in the Museo Sacro at the Vatican).

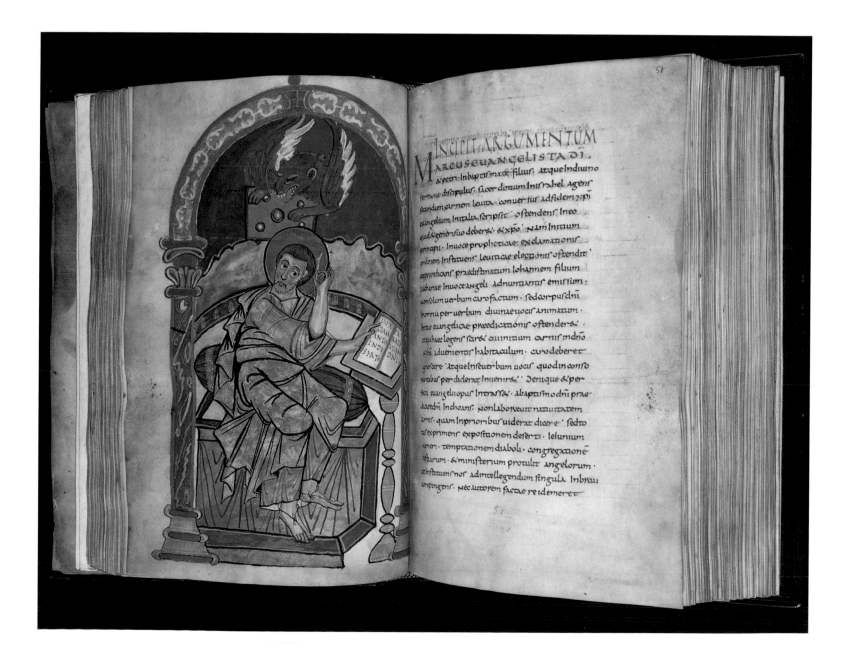

56

Petrus Lombardus Super Psalmos
(Peter Lombard's Commentary
on the Psalms)

Manuscript on vellum, 355 × 240mm, ff.197, double columns of 48 lines.

Bound in the thirteenth century, with the addition of a Mosan *champlevé* enamel panel depicting the *Crucifixion*, set with small turquoises, and surrounded by a border of six long metal panels of similar decorative work, with four metal disks at the inner corners.

Bought by Lord Lindsay from Thomas Boone in October 1861 for £80.

REFERENCES: James, 1921, no.6; F. Steenbock, *Der kirchliche Prachteinband im frühen Mittelalter*, Berlin, 1965, pp.222–3, no.121; Barker, 1978, p.225.

LENT BY THE JOHN RYLANDS UNIVERSITY
LIBRARY OF MANCHESTER

This manuscript was written in the twelfth century by two expert scribes, in early gothic script, for the Cistercian monastery of Himmerod in the Rhineland. The text is the commentary on the Psalms of Peter Lombard (c.1100–c.1160), an Italian who was first professor and later, in 1159, Bishop of Paris. His *Sententiae* were required reading in all monasteries observing the Benedictine rule, and this volume was written out for use at Himmerod, probably in the monastery's scriptorium.

57

Missal of Henry of Chichester

Manuscript on vellum, 327 × 203mm, ff.258, two columns of 31–40 lines to the page.

Bought by Lord Lindsay in February 1860 for £126 from Thomas Kerslake of Bristol, who had acquired it from 'a church near Torquay'.

REFERENCES: James, 1921, no.24; A.E.J. Hollaender, 'The Sarum Illuminator and his School', *Wiltshire Archaeological Magazine*, I, 1942–4, pp.230ff; Barker, 1978, pp.203–4.

LENT BY THE JOHN RYLANDS UNIVERSITY LIBRARY OF MANCHESTER

Missals were the books in which the central text of the mass was accompanied by the special collects, epistles and gospels for Sundays and feast-days throughout the year. This manuscript was written about 1250-60 in English *textura* in varying sizes, with plain chant on four-line stave, and illuminated, perhaps in the scriptorium of the new Cathedral at Salisbury, for Henry of Chichester, precentor of Crediton. It was given by him, probably before 1264, to Exeter Cathedral, where it was listed among gifts made by him in or before 1277, including fourteen missals, of which this is probably item seven: *bonum notatum cum tropariis cum multis ymaginibus subtilibus de auro in canone* ('a fine one with musical notation for the tropes and many fine gilt pictures in the canon of the mass'). The binding of alum-tawed hide over wooden boards, with remains of strap and pin fastening, is probably contemporary.

58

Psalter

Manuscript on vellum, 260 × 171mm, ff.169, 19 lines to the page.

Bought by Lord Lindsay from Bernard Quaritch in September 1869 for £145 1s; previously in the collections of the Manchester antiquary James Crossley, and Sir Henry Mainwaring of Peover Hall, to which he succeeded in 1798.

REFERENCES: James, 1921, no.22; R. Branner, *Manuscript Painting in Paris during the Reign of St Louis*, Berkeley, 1977, pp.45–7; Barker, 1978, p.243.

LENT BY THE JOHN RYLANDS UNIVERSITY LIBRARY OF MANCHESTER

Written about 1225–30 in a fine *textura* hand by two accomplished professional scribes. Illuminated by the 'atelier of the Vienna Moralized Bibles', which supplied the royal and noble market in Paris in the early thirteenth-century, with full-page pictures (some missing) and smaller illustrations to every psalm. Such books were produced for important persons, either for private devotion or to accompany liturgical use. This manuscript bears the later signature ('Royne Jahanne') of Jeanne de Navarre (died 1437), wife of Jean de Montfort, Duke of Brittany (died 1399) and then of Henry IV of England. The present binding of blind-stamped calf over wooden boards with clasps (missing) probably dates from her ownership.

59

Nicolas de Lyra, Postilla Super Bibliam (Nicolas de Lyra's Commentary on the Complete Text of the Bible)

Manuscript on vellum, 425 × 280mm, ff.305, 228, 202, two columns of 68 lines.

Bought by Lord Lindsay from T. & W. Boone in February 1866 for £200, and bound in morocco about this time.

REFERENCES: James, 1921, nos.29–31; Barker, 1978, p.225.

LENT BY THE JOHN RYLANDS UNIVERSITY LIBRARY OF MANCHESTER

Written and finished at the Franciscan convent at Pesaro by the scribe Ugolino Marini Gibertuzzi of Sarnano in April 1402, at the behest of Pandolfo III Malatesta (1370-1427), and illuminated throughout. It was inherited by the Gonzaga family, probably by bequest from Pandolfo III, Archbishop of Patras, to Paola Malatesta, and was presented by Lodovico Gonzaga (1414–78), Marquess of Mantua, to the Franciscan convent there on 24 March 1469. The Commentary of Nicolas de Lyra on the Bible was a popular text in the fifteenth century.

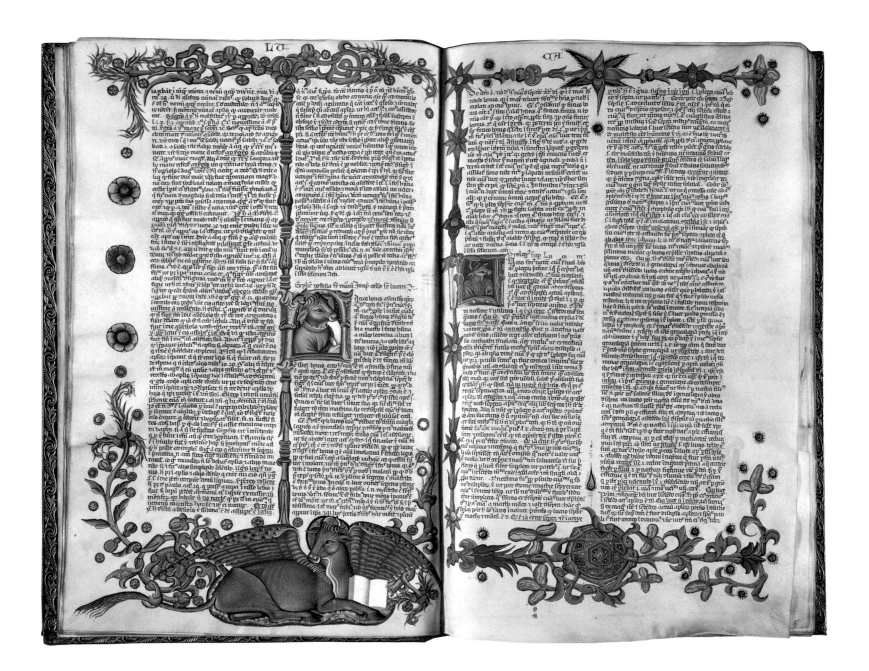

60

Johannes Cassianus, Collationes Patrum et Instituta Coenobiorum (John Cassian's Dialogues with the Pious Fathers of Egypt, and Rules for the Conduct of Life for Monks)

Manuscript on vellum, 279 × 208mm, ff.283, 36 lines to the page.

Bought by Bernard Quaritch at the Libri sale in March 1859 for £13 5s., and sold by him to Lord Lindsay for £20 the following month; bound, probably for Libri, in blue morocco by C. Smith.

REFERENCES: James, 1921, no.49; Barker,1978, p.176.

LENT BY THE JOHN RYLANDS UNIVERSITY LIBRARY OF MANCHESTER

Written in the second quarter of the fifteenth century in a fine upright humanistic minuscule, probably in the Veneto, where it was also illuminated. The text deals with the lives and acts of the monks and hermits of the Thebaid, a subject dear to Lord Lindsay since his own journey to Egypt and the Holy Land. Lindsay also acquired two cassone panels on the same theme (cat.nos.11 and 12), which vividly illustrate, in particular, the monks' temptations by and combats with devils, a subject referred to extensively in the first of these texts.

61

Horae ('The Mary Queen of Scots Book of Hours')

Manuscript on vellum, 68 × 46mm, ff.253, 16 lines to the page.

Bought by Lord Lindsay at the André B. Knox sale in August 1872, on commission through Bernard Quaritch, for £36 6s., and subsequently bound in green velvet by Hayday.

REFERENCES: James, 1921, no.21; Barker, 1978, p.247.

LENT BY THE JOHN RYLANDS UNIVERSITY LIBRARY OF MANCHESTER

Written about the year 1500 in *littera moderna* script in Flanders, with Flemish illumination by a professional atelier. The original patron is unknown, but it was later owned by Mary, Queen of Scots. From the thirteenth century onwards, the Hours of the Virgin, with other texts, became the universal book of personal piety for lay people, and noble and royal personages had finely illuminated copies made for their own use. This tiny volume contains twenty full-page miniatures and twenty-four smaller pictures of saints and other subjects. It contains two inscriptions in Mary's hand: 'Mon Dieu confondez mes ennemys M' ('My Lord defeat my enemies, M[ary]'; on f.113); and 'Dieu vivant mon seul Juge olyez mes plainctes & mes gemissementz' ('Living God, my sole judge, hear my pleas and my groans'; on f.124).

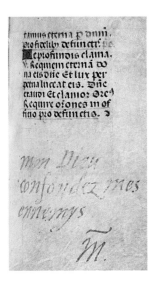

62

The Colonna Missal (first volume)

Manuscript on vellum, 370 × 260mm, ff.108.

Bought by Lord Lindsay from Thomas Boone in June 1868 for £1500, who had it from Thomas Payne of Payne and Foss and believed it came 'from the Colonna Sciarra branch of the family'.

REFERENCES: James, 1921, no.32; Barker,1978, pp.225–6; J.J.G. Alexander, *The Towneley Lectionary*, London, 1997, p.39.

LENT BY THE JOHN RYLANDS UNIVERSITY LIBRARY OF MANCHESTER

Written in a large accomplished *littera moderna* script and illuminated in Rome for Cardinal Pompeo Colonna (died 1532), but not complete at the time of his death. This is the first of the six volumes of the Missal that were once in the Bibliotheca Lindesiana (a seventh volume, formerly in the Doheny collection, is dated 21 May 1539). The illumination, in Renaissance classical style, is attributable to Vincenzo Raimondi (Vincent Raymond de Lodève) and other artists. The exhibited illustration to the Mass of St John the Baptist exhibits an astonishing panoply of Egyptian motifs, including statues of Apis, Serapis and Osiris, sphinxes, obelisks with hieroglyphics, Trajan's Column, etc., with a central medallion of the Baptist's father, Zacharias the priest. The first and seventh volumes were bound at the time and elaborately gilt with the Colonna device, a column, by 'Maestro Luigi' (Luigi de Gava or de Gradi), the latter presumably when written, the former slightly later. The remaining five volumes are in seventeenth-century bindings.

E uen
te ma
ri mee
vocat
me do
minus
nomie
meo is
et posu

it os meam ut gladium
acutum sub tegumento
manus sue protexit me
et posuit me quasi sagit

DIVO
POMPEIO

CARDINALI
COLVMNÆ

Abbreviated References

ARSLAN, 1960
W. Arslan, I Bassano, 2 vols., Milan, 1960.

BARKER, 1978
N. Barker, Bibliotheca Lindesiana, 2nd edition, London, 1978.

BASEL, 1974
Basel, Kunstmuseum, Lukas Cranach: Gemälde, Zeichnungen, Druckgraphik, exhibition catalogue edited by D. Koepplin and T. Falk, 2 vols., 1974.

BELLOSI, 1974
L. Bellosi, Buffalmacco e il Trionfo della Morte, Turin, 1974..

BERENSON, 1894
B. Berenson, The Venetian Painters of the Renaissance, New York, 1894.

BERENSON, 1907
B. Berenson, The North Italian Painters of the Renaissance, New York and London, 1907.

BERENSON, 1932
B. Berenson, Italian Pictures of the Renaissance, Oxford, 1932.

BERENSON, 1957
B. Berenson, Italian Pictures of the Renaissance: Venetian School, 2 vols., London, 1957.

BERENSON, 1963
B. Berenson, Italian Pictures of the Renaissance: Florentine School, 2 vols., London, 1963.

BERENSON, 1968
B. Berenson, Italian Pictures of the Renaissance: Central Italian and North Italian Schools, 3 vols., London, 1968.

BISOGNI, 1972
F. Bisogni, 'Contributo per un problema ferrarese' in Paragone, 265, 1972, pp.69–79.

BOSKOVITS, 1971
M. Boskovits, 'Notes sur Giovanni da Milano' in Revue de l'Art, II, 1971, pp.55–8.

BOSKOVITS, 1975
M. Boskovits, Pittura Fiorentina alla vigilia del Rinascimento 1370 – 1400, Florence, 1975.

BOSKOVITS, 1990
M. Boskovits, Thyssen-Bornemisza Collection: Early Italian Painting 1290–1470, London, 1990.

BOUCHER, 1991
B. Boucher, The Sculpture of Jacopo Sansovino, 2 vols., New Haven and London, 1991.

BRIGSTOCKE, 1981
H. Brigstocke, 'Lord Lindsay and the Sketches of the History of Christian Art', Bulletin of the John Rylands University Library of Manchester, 64, 1, 1981, pp.27–60.

BRIGSTOCKE, 1982
H. Brigstocke, 'Lord Lindsay as a Collector', Bulletin of the John Rylands University Library of Manchester, 64, 2, 1982, pp.287–333.

BRIGSTOCKE, 1993
H. Brigstocke, Italian and Spanish Paintings in the National Gallery of Scotland, 2nd revised edition, Edinburgh, 1993.

CALLMANN, 1974
E. Callmann, Apollonio di Giovanni, Oxford, 1974.

CROWE AND CAVALCASELLE, 1864
J. A. Crowe and G. B. Cavalcaselle, A New History of Painting in Italy, London, 1864.

CROWE AND CAVALCASELLE, 1908
J. A. Crowe and G. B. Cavalcaselle, A History of Painting in Italy, edited by R. Langton Douglas, 6 vols., London, 1908.

DAVIES AND GORDON, 1988
M. Davies, revised by D. Gordon, National Gallery Catalogues: The Early Italian Schools Before 1400, London, 1988.

DICTIONARY OF ART, 1996
The Macmillan - Grove Dictionary of Art, edited by J. Turner, 34 vols., London and New York, 1996.

FEHM, 1986
S. Fehm, Luca di Tommè: A Sienese Fourteenth Century Painter, Carbondale and Edwardsville, 1986.

FERRARA, 1998
Ferrara, Museo d'Arte Moderna e Contemporanea, New York, Metropolitan Museum, and Los Angeles, J. Paul Getty Museum, Dosso Dossi, Court Painter in Renaissance Ferrara, exhibition catalogue edited by P. Humfrey and M. Lucco, 1998-9.

FIESOLE, 1998
Fiesole, Basilica di Sant'Alessandro, I della Robbia e l'arta nuova della scultura invetriata, exhibition catalogue edited by G. Gentilini, 1998.

FLORENCE, 1992
Florence, Palazzo Strozzi, Maestri e Botteghi: Pittura a Firenze alla fine del Quattrocento, exhibition catalogue edited by M. Gregori et al., 1992-3.

FRIEDLÄNDER, 1969
M. J. Friedländer, Early Netherlandish Painting, IV: Hugo van der Goes, Leiden and Brussels, 1969.

GENTILINI, 1993
G. Gentilini, *I Della Robbia: La scultura invetriata nel Rinascimento*, 2 vols., Florence, 1993.

GIACOMOTTI, 1974
J. Giacomotti, *Catalogue des maioliques des musées nationaux*, Paris, 1974.

JAMES, 1921
M. R. James, *A Descriptive Catalogue of the Latin Manuscripts in the John Rylands Library at Manchester*, Manchester, 1921 (2nd edition with additions by F. Taylor, Munich, 1980).

KECKS, 1998
R. G. Kecks, *Domenico Ghirlandaio*, Florence, 1998.

LINDSAY, 1847
A. W. (Lord) Lindsay, *Sketches of the History of Christian Art*, 3 vols., London, 1847 (sometimes abbreviated in the text of this catalogue as 'Sketches')

LONDON, 1893
London, New Gallery, *Early Italian Art from 1300 to 1550*, exhibition catalogue, 1893-4.

LONDON, 1904
London, Burlington Fine Arts Club, *Pictures of Siena and Objects of Art*, exhibition catalogue, 1904.

LONDON, 1930
London, Royal Academy, *Exhibition of Italian Art 1200-1900*, 1930.

MILAN, 1991
Milan, Museo Poldi Pezzoli, *Le Muse e il Principe*, exhibition catalogue edited by A. Mottola Molfino and M. Natale, 2 vols., 1991.

NEW YORK, 1988
New York, Metropolitan Museum of Art, *Painting in Renaissance Siena 1420-1500*, exhibition catalogue by K. Christiansen, L.B. Kanter and C. Brandon Strehlke, 1988-9.

POPE-HENNESSY, 1964
J. Pope-Hennessy, assisted by R. Lightbown, *Catalogue of Italian Sculpture in the Victoria and Albert Museum*, 3 vols., London, 1964.

RACKHAM, 1977
B. Rackham, *Victoria and Albert Museum: Catalogue of Italian Maiolica*, edited by J. V. G. Mallet, 2 vols., London, 1977.

RIO, 1836
A. F. Rio, *De La Poésie Chrétienne*, Paris, 1836.

SCHUBRING, 1915
P. Schubring, *Cassoni: Truhen und Truhenbilder der italienischen Frührenaissance*, Leipzig, 1915.

TRENTO, 1999
Trento, Castello del Buonconsiglio, *'La bellissima maniera': Alessandro Vittoria e la scultura veneta del Cinquecento*, exhibition catalogue edited by A. Bacchi, L. Camerlengo, and M. Leithe-Jasper, 1999.

VAN MARLE, 1923–38
R. van Marle, *The Development of the Italian Schools of Painting*, 19 vols., The Hague, 1923-38.

VERCELLI, 1995
Vercelli, Museo Civico Borgogna, *Bernardino Lanino*, exhibition catalogue edited by P. Astrua and G. Romano, 1995.

WAAGEN, 1854
G. Waagen, *Treasures of Art in Great Britain*, 3 vols., London, 1854.